TRADITIONAL MUSIC:
WHOSE MUSIC?

To Sadie & Sam

Best Wishes

Peter NacDamiel

June, 1992

ACKNOWLEDGEMENTS

Co-operation North is extremely grateful to the Arts Council of Northern Ireland and An Chomhairle Ealaión for drawing up the conference programme, and for part-funding the conference. We also wish to thank the CCRU for authorising a European Regional Development Fund Grant towards the cost of producing this publication.

Published by the Institute of Irish Studies, 1992.
Copyright Co-operation North, 1992.

ISBN 0 948297 03 4

Printed by W.G. Baird Ltd, Antrim

Traditional Music:
Whose Music?

Edited by Peter McNamee

Proceedings of a Co-operation North Conference

1991

The Institute of Irish Studies
The Queen's University of Belfast

CONTENTS

PREFACE

The need to hold a conference on traditional music, putting the question '*Whose* Music?', became increasingly evident due to a whole series of inter-related factors: face-to-face contacts made with many people involved and interested in the music, personal experiences gleaned over the years, the 'cultural traditions' debate which has been proceeding apace within Northern Ireland; all coupled with Co-operation North's cross-border remit to contribute to a greater dialogue between, and understanding about, the primary duality of cultural traditions in Ireland. The conference brochure posited the idea that 'Traditional music, in all its eclectic forms, means many things to many people, but it belongs to everyone, including musicians.' This multi-faceted idea was put to the test in the panel sessions which took place on the Friday, in the Open Forum which took place on the Saturday morning; and the deliberations were then ably and eloquently concluded and commented upon by Michael Longley in the final Summary.

Co-operation North intended this to be an opportunity to look at, to explore, and to discuss the origins and the many and varied influences which have acted upon and shaped the development of traditional music on this island, in the hope that such a discussion would make an important – and a much-needed – contribution to a greater awareness of both the nature of the music and its effects upon people today. As it was, the conference succeeded in exploring the origins of traditional music; first, with a wide-ranging analysis from Sean Corcoran and a thought-provoking account by Tom Munnelly, and then comparatively, with frank insights to religious attitudes combined with personal recollections of growing up with the song tradition in the Outer Hebrides from Flora MacNeil and Mary Jane Campbell. Piers Hellawell, with a background in classical music, drew everyone's attention to some of the contemporary influences upon classical music, not the least being traditional music, and he counselled us to be 'borrowers', not 'burglars'. David Bushe's was a brisk and laconic voice, claiming that 'Ulster

Orange music' is 'what stirs your heart', an attribute which binds people together.

Two quite different perspectives on traditional music followed. First of all, traditional musicians themselves further stimulated the debate with individual accounts of how they became involved with the music. Paddy Glackin reminded everyone of the urban context, of the cultural complexities thrown up by coming to the music within the confines of the city. Paddy's experience centred upon Dublin in the 1960s; Desi Wilkinson's upon Belfast in the 1970s. Leslie Bingham, 'from an Orange background', explained how the pull between self-acknowledged background and the playing of traditional music was accomplished because he 'enjoyed the music so much'. Richard Parkes put flesh on the bones of some of the points raised by Sean Corcoran with a timely reminder of the sharing of jigs and reels, emphasising the cross-channel give-and-take of Scottish and Irish traditions, the distinction being that pipe bands closely correlate with tribal identity in Northern Ireland, but not nearly to the same extent in Scotland. Mairéad Ní Dhomhnaill echoed many of the homely sentiments expressed by Flora MacNeil, having been 'surrounded' by songs from a very early age, having had them passed on, and now as guarantor she is an indispensable link in the chain.

The final conference session of the day explored the public perception of the music, picking up and pursuing many of the themes raised in the preceding session. Cathal Goan and Dermot McLaughlin focused upon the frequently unhappy juxtaposition between the natural and immediate expression of the music, and the often contrived, unnatural, 'you-stand-here' mentality of the media, especially television. Radio fared much better! Tony McAuley, Andy Crockart and Riobard Mac Góráin concentrated upon the cultural fissures already present, the role of the media in televising events, and the need to be aware of the first whilst engaged in the second.

Ciarán Mac Mathúna reminded everyone of two things: that the music was held up to a middle-class, urban-based ridicule during the 1950s and '60s; and that, having weathered that storm, there was then a danger of it being subjected to political pressures in the 1970s, subsumed as an adjunct to Republicanism.

In the evening, debate gave way to entertainment. Tom McDevitte, otherwise known as 'Barney McCool', stood up and regaled the audience with his wit and charm. Then it was the turn of the musicians who treated everyone to some outstanding solo performances in the concert which followed, with fiddles and flutes, the Scottish pipes, and songs. This was surely the practical side of all that had been discussed during the day, and as such, it would be unfair to single out any one musician for special praise; everyone was at their best. Finally, the grand finale of fiddles and flutes was a marvellous exposé of the very vibrant nature of traditional music itself, so aptly expressing in sound and sentiment the references made to the 'camaraderie' of the music – the sessions – by Desi Wilkinson and others earlier in the day.

The Open Forum took place on the Saturday morning, with delegates having the opportunity to follow up on many of the points raised in the panel discussions of the previous day. Two central themes emerged: firstly, how many traditions are there?; secondly, how and why did the 'revival' of the 1960s come about? How individual musicians have responded to both themes was partly explored in terms of, what Fintan Vallely felt was, the 'onus' being 'put on us' to contribute to the debate, and partly in terms of society's need to understand that musicians are individuals who play music before they are members of organisations.

Is there one mainstream music tradition offering a common parentage to both Orange and Green, two mutually exclusive traditions, or is traditional music the inherited property of everyone (or, as David Bushe said, ' . . . if there are a thousand traditions, 998 of them don't count: there's only two that count!')? If we accept that there are two traditions, how can we ensure their respective and undiluted integrities so that they can, as Michael Longley noted, ' . . . prosper, be themselves and benefit from each other'? Again, if we accept two traditions, must we also accept, as David Bushe suggested, that they are 'ethnically' diverse? The likely pitfalls of superimposing ethnic origin on the music were raised by Cathal Goan: ' . . . the problem of talking about cultural traditions as opposed to musical traditions . . . '

The candle of traditional music was rekindled with a revival in interest taking place in the 1960s: was this a spontaneous cultural renewal of commitment to the music on the part of the musicians themselves, free of all institutional control and direction, or was it due to the work of an organisation like *Comhaltas Ceolteóirí Éireann* (Irish Cultural Movement: founded in 1951 to promote Irish traditional music, song, dance and language)? Cathal Goan reminded us that, '*Comhaltas* is a huge organisation', and that,

'Most young people playing traditional music in Ireland have come into contact with music through *Comhaltas*.' Fintan Vallely reminded us that, '*Comhaltas* is not an organisation. *Comhaltas* is only a collection of individuals at any one point in time.' These are conflicting interpretations. Unfortunately, *Comhaltas Ceolteóirí Éireann* were unable to send a delegate to the conference.

Michael Longley delivered a very perceptive – and, in parts, a very moving – summing up of the two days of conference, and his Summary at the end of this report contains his short poem dedicated to Brian O'Donnell, '*Fleadh*', which avails of a variety of musical instruments as the inspiration for the poet's unparalleled insight. It is worthwhile quoting Michael's peroration: ' . . . we are talking about something that is intimate and at the same time vast, and we have in Northern Ireland . . . the uniquely rich confluence of English and Irish and Scottish songs and tunes; and it is that very richness which produces political problems, social complexities.'

Both the proceedings of the two-day conference and the Friday evening's concert were televised by UTV for an hour-long programme which was transmitted on 26th November, 1990: *Fiddles and Flutes: Whose Music?* UTV's News Release for the programme summed up the rationale of the conference as follows: 'There is a perception that traditional music is Catholic music: despite the fact that it is enjoyed and performed by many from a Protestant background . . . For the first time musicians, broadcasters, collectors and those interested in cultural traditions have come together for a wide-ranging debate on the subject.' The television programme included some discussions which had taken place outside the conference venue, but at the same time – and because an hour-long programme cannot cover everything discussed at a two-day conference – there were some aspects of the conference, such as the second panel discussion on 'An Island Experience', which were not included. *Fiddles and Flutes* was directed by Steve Ward and produced by Michael Beattie. It was entered at the 1991 Celtic Film and Television Festival held in Inverness.

Co-operation North owes special thanks to Ciaran Carson and Sean Corcoran of the Arts Council of Northern Ireland and Dermot McLaughlin of *An Chomhairle Ealaion* for all their considered advice and practical assistance in organising the conference. Thanks are also due to Aodán Mac Póilin of the Ultach Trust for checking the spelling of Gaelic words in the transcripts, to Michael Longley for

his very helpful comments on the completed draft, to Bob Galway
for proof-reading the final draft, and to Nicola Hall for transcribing
the sound-recordings so meticulously, given the deadline she had
to work to.

Peter McNamee

CONFERENCE CHAIRPERSON'S INTRODUCTION

Tommy Fegan, Deputy Chief Executive, Co-operation North

You are all very welcome, both from the North and the South, and particularly people who have travelled from abroad to attend this conference. The conference is a very significant milestone for Co-operation North. In the eleven years since our inception we have been developing programmes to bring people together over a wide range of issues, such as the social, the economic, the educational, and through school links. But this particular conference marks the beginning of a new programme, entitled the 'Cultural Traditions Programme', which aims to generate dialogue and contribute to existing dialogue about the issues that can actually be divisive in society and the issues that are manipulated, and perhaps misunderstood: things like religion, sport, and, in this particular case, art.

We feel that Irish traditional music, because it has been enjoying such great popularity world-wide, has been overlooked by a lot of people who are, maybe, not particularly interested in it and that it has been misunderstood; and the influences that have come to bear on Irish traditional music, we feel, are also at the heart of some of the issues that give rise to some of the problems that we are currently experiencing. So, we are particularly delighted that the panel of speakers here today, and the panels that are to follow during the next two days, have agreed that the issue is of such a serious and urgent nature that they have given freely of their time to come along and help generate this dialogue.

I have to express a note of regret that *Comhaltas Ceolteóirí Éireann* were unable to send a delegate. Co-operation North approached *Comhaltas* at the very outset because we recognised the tremendous contribution they have made in the resurgence of Irish traditional music over the last thirty to forty years, and I think the conference will be all the poorer for their absence. However, if there are members of *Comhaltas* here I would like to say that they are particularly welcome, and we would look forward to a fuller and vigorous discussion on all aspects of the programme which you have before you.

So, without further ado I will hand you over to a man who is well known to all of you here. Sean Corcoran has been a collector, a practitioner, and a researcher into songs of various traditional backgrounds over this past number of years. He has given freely of his time to help Co-operation North put this conference together, and we are very indebted to him.

PANEL ONE

WHAT IS TRADITIONAL MUSIC?

Panel Chairperson: Sean Corcoran
                                   Traditional Music Researcher

Panel Members: Piers Hellawell
                                   Classical Musician

David Bushe
                                   Ulster Society

Tom Munnelly
                                   Collector of Traditional Songs

SEAN CORCORAN: PANEL CHAIRPERSON

Traditional Music Researcher

This is a fairly unique conference, the first of its kind; hopefully not the last. Normally these topics are debated by musicians themselves in the back rooms of public houses, or sitting on a wall at a *Fleadh*, or places like that; or else they are debated by academics among themselves. So, this is unique in that it is the first time this topic has been opened to the general public. At the moment I am doing research for the Arts Council of Northern Ireland. I spent many years travelling the back roads of Ireland recording the song tradition, singers mainly, and I was also interested in a certain amount of the instrumental tradition to be found in Sligo, Leitrim, and Fermanagh; also the fife and lambeg tradition around Cullybackey, County Antrim. These are purely my own personal views. I am speaking on behalf of no organisation.

We will begin at the very beginning: 'What is Traditional Music?' is the title of this section of the seminar. I suppose the best way to find out what it is is to stay around until this evening when the concert is on and you can hear the real thing. Theory can never match practice. However, the word itself, 'tradition', is a strange word. In English it survives, to quote one definition, as a description of a 'general process of handing down, but there is also a very strong and often a predominant sense of disentailing respect and duty.' That is a definition by Raymond Williams. So, there is an emphasis on the conservative aspect of the music, but my own experience is that while the form may be conservative, the structures fairly permanent, the actual content may be quite innovative, and often surreal.

All musics have their own tradition. In this sense orchestral music, for instance, would be in a sense almost more traditional than Irish traditional music in that the style of performance and the very limited range of periods covered in orchestral music, are very, very traditional indeed. This idea of tradition is also used socially quite a lot in various forms in the construction of ideologies. I will talk about this later on in more detail, but just to throw out a few examples: the kilt in Scotland, I am told, is a relatively recent introduction; a British Army invention in its modern form. The idea of clan tartans is also an invention. I am told that much of the ritual concerning the British Royal Family is fairly recent; also the ritual of post-colonial Africa. A lot of the ritual attached to kingship in Africa is relatively recent; a post-colonial invention. Coming closer to home, the revived Irish harp is very much an invention. The traditions in Irish dancing, that form which was recently described as 'the kind of dancing that wee girls who wear costumes with the *Book of Kells* on it do'; that sort of dancing, I will show in some depth later on how that is very much an invention.

It is interesting that among the singers and performers themselves, there is no word used colloquially for the kind of music they perform and sing. Now, 'traditional' has certainly become the most popular term over the recent past number of years, but in general singers would not say, 'I sing traditional songs.' They would never say, 'I sing folk-songs.' That means something else altogether in their minds. They would say something like 'singing old songs', and they would use that term even if the songs are quite newly made but made in the traditional style. As far as I know, it is interesting that in Irish itself there is no colloquially known word for this kind of music. *Sean-nós* singing in Connemara is, to my knowledge, a relatively recent coining. So, at least the term 'traditional' has one aspect to it that is relevant; it stresses the processes involved in the music, and I think that the secret of traditional music, ultimately, has to do with the processes involved in its production and creation, and it is those processes that are of a wider interest, a wider importance.

So, we come to another definition that is often used: 'folk'. I have a lovely quotation here from Kevin Danagher, a great scholar and writer from the Irish Folklore Commission. He says that, 'It is unfortunate that the recent residuum of this tradition should be designated "folklore", with all of that word's connotations; on the one hand, of mental slumming among the lower orders and lesser breeds, on the other hand, of pseudoscience and wild theorising. We should remember that in the Irish context "folklore" is a mistranslation of *bealoideas* which means, literally, oral instruction; a word of much wider and much apter sense.' Going further afield, I thought I would give you a quotation from Brecht. As Germany has recently re-united, I thought it would be appropriate, and also to show you that things are much the same as at home. Also, it is one of the nicest insights into the actual processes of tradition, or that kind of popular song, that I have come across. It is a lengthy quotation but worthwhile reading. He says, in an article entitled 'Where I Have Learned My Craft':

I was relatively late in getting to know any folk-songs apart from one or two songs by Goethe and Heine, which were sung at odd occasions, which I didn't really know to count as popular songs or not since the populous had no hand in them. Not even contributing the slightest modifications, it is almost as if in remoulding the popular heritage, the great writers and musicians of the progressive bourgeoisie had robbed the populous proper of its language. What I used to hear people singing in my childhood were cheap hits and interminable ditties about noble robbers. In these, certainly, there remained echoes of an earlier tradition, however blurred and debased they may be, and the singers would still add words of their own. The women workers in the nearby paper factory would sometimes fail to remember all the verses of a song and make improvised transitions from which much could be learned. Their attitude towards the songs was also instructive: they never let themselves be naïvely carried away. They would sing individual verses of entire songs with a certain irony, putting quotation marks, as it where, [lovely phrase] around a lot that was cheap, exaggerated and unreal. They were not all that far removed from those highly educated compilers of the Homeric epics who were inspired by naïvety without being themselves naïve.

In the same vein, this also has an application to what is normally called folk music in the run-of-the-mill media nowadays. He says, 'Modern pseudo folk-songs are, for many, discouraging examples. To start with, because of their artificial simplicity. Where the folk-song uses simple means to say something complicated, the modern imitators are saying something simple or simple-minded in a simple way. The people have no wish to be *folk*.' Now, that has a bearing on the use of the term 'folk', 'folklore'. In modern-day scholarship, it is very much of an Anglo-Saxon revival of the mid-nineteenth century; where, with words like 'astronomy' it was suggested that they use 'starlore', 'earthlore', and so on. They wanted to Anglo-Saxonise the language, and I think the word 'folk-song' was coined around 1870. But since the word 'folklore' itself was coined around 1846, folklorists themselves have had terrible difficulty in knowing exactly how to define the word.

This has a bearing on the way this culture, this music culture, is seen. Most of these older definitions of folklore emphasised older elements surviving into a strange and new present. Hence, the songs were not seen as a living process, but almost as archaeological artefacts; and singers then were not conscious creators and re-creators of a musical idiom: they were passive transmitters. So, the folk-song collectors were simply interested in going out into the field and bringing back an artefact (a song), which could be taken to be slightly like Victorian butterfly-collecting, where you get a living butterfly, you bung it into the killing bottle, you mount, and then you begin the classification of the creature.

Folk music has the other connotation of defining the music in terms of the social classes who practise this music; so then, you ask people who are musicologists, 'If that is folk music what is the opposite?' and they say, 'Well, art music', which immediately implies that folk music is not artistic. I have got a lovely wee word for it, 'WEEM': Western European Elite Music! Many of the music traditions, say for instance from the Far East and so on; they define different areas of music so that there is the music of religious monasteries, there is the music of wandering theatrical groups, there is the music of the aristocracy, the music of the folk and the common people, and so on. They can actually separate the music into different and clearly defined social groupings, and I think that, perhaps, this is the way we should be looking at things here as well.

This is something which is never stressed in collections: it is extraordinary that in all my time collecting and looking back to the older collections and so on, the social class of 99.99 per cent of the performers tended to be rural, farm labourers and small farmers; so that, essentially, this music is now of the recent past. Obviously, we know from historical research that something like this music, certainly the same song texts and so on, that the same melodies were used in an urban situation in the last century and the century before that. But for now and the recent past, it is a reflection, a musical reflection, of the world view of a specific social class.

Is it popular music? Before the word 'folk' was used for this music, they simply used the word 'popular'. Nowadays 'popular' is generally used for music which is only popular in consumption, so I would like to make the definition that this is the only music which we have that is popularly generated. It is the only music which is distinctive. It may be from here, from there; from Antrim or from Kerry. It goes through a process where the initial sources, maybe from outside this country or maybe from outside that social class, leave us in no doubt that the regeneration of this music and the re-invention of it, as Brecht spoke of it earlier on in referring to the factory workers, is certainly popularly generated. Whereas, you know that the music you hear on the mass media, which is pop music, ultimately has its source in New York or London.

I played pieces of different music from different sources for a well-known musician once. One comment this musician made (I played him some Beethoven) was that, 'It's very nice, but it takes an awful long while getting in on the tune!' So, how was this music actually different to 'elite' music? Does it have a different aesthetic and why should we point out the differences at all? I think it is very important to point these differences out because I think the processes involved are totally different, and the aesthetic involved is a different aesthetic from that of orchestral music or so-called Western art music. This is the most difficult one of all to analyse and explain. I will put it like this: I was once asked by a Cavan man, 'What does an olive taste like?' (it is the sort of question a Cavan man would ask you), and I really couldn't tell him. That suddenly set me thinking, 'If I and a Greek eat the same olive, what do we taste?' Obviously, what we perceive of the taste is going to be different, and more important, the social overtones that go with that taste will also be different. I would be thinking of exotic holidays; perhaps he would be thinking of a homely feeling. Maybe he would be thinking of back-breaking hours spent out on the olive groves.

I say this because, as I mentioned earlier on, as part of my project studying music in Fermanagh, we played different pieces, different sources of music to very, very fine traditional musicians. I mentioned the comment they made about Beethoven earlier on: a lot of exotic music, they simply couldn't comprehend at all! Music is not an international language; it really needs to be understood on its own terms. Each idiom of music is a totally different idiom, much the same as the language. Anyway, I mixed certain players from different parts of the country. They could very easily recognise other regional styles, and they often recognised exactly who the musician was; they knew his style intimately. Occasionally I played tapes of young people who were beginning to learn, and they would say, 'He is getting on well', and so on; and occasionally

I played two tapes of very competent classical musicians who also played some Irish music. The 'classical' musicians in question are household names: they are obviously highly skilled masters of their own musical idioms and would have very receptive 'ears'. Yet, their attempts to 'reproduce' Irish traditional music sounded to the older players like the strivings of incompetent youngsters!

Which brings me to the point: what do we hear when we hear this music? I am not saying to people that there is no way that you can understand this music if you are not steeped in it from birth, but it is the old question, 'Do you have to be black to sing the blues, do you have to be native-speaking Irish to sing *sean-nós?*' There is a major problem there, a problem of perception.

How is it different? Well, I am sure that any of you who have read any of this topic are familiar with these aspects of the music. The tonal system is totally different. The tonal system of an Irish fiddler doesn't exist on a piano. The timbre of the music and the idea and context of performance are totally different. I was very privileged, here in Fermanagh, to be involved in many instances of *ceili*-ing, where people simply dropped into houses in the evenings and sat there and played a few tunes, and so on. The songs and the tunes exist, not as separate items, but they exist in a total continuum, and often when you take them out of that continuum they seem to lose all sense and all reality. It is a bit like a fish taken out of water; all you can do is bang them on the head and disembowel them, and that is often what songs on a concert platform sound like. As I go to *Fleadh* competitions and see the singing competitions, it sounds like fish out of water.

The final point I want to make is that this music in this country has been picked upon, and has been used as part of a construction of various ideologies. There is a lovely word here which I must use: 'mediation' (it is necessary to use some words like this because they have been honed down over the years in debate and discussion). It essentially means that certain social forces come between a reality and the social consciousness at the end of it. The mediation of the musical reality which is there often begins, for instance, with collectors who only select from a single repertoire certain songs which sound to them appropriate or ancient. Many of the great *sean-nós* singers (Elizabeth Crone was a good example), would have extraordinary songs in Irish and then the most mundane, modern music-hall songs mixed together in their repertoire. Often when you look at some of the early collectors, e.g.

Petrie and Joyce and so on, what actual information do you get
from these collections? What you get is almost a stick insect, a little
stick-man picture; it is as if instead of having a photograph you had
simply a stick outline; so you vaguely see the outline of the melody
but very, very little else about how it was produced, how it was
performed, and so on. Even the actual transcriptions these men
used at the time were quite skeletal. Now we can only imagine how
these songs were performed because the very same melodies are
still sung these days. Most of the tune structures in the older
collections are still sung, and from the modern performance we
can reconstruct from Petrie and Joyce the ways in which these
songs were performed in the last century.

Finally, a major note of controversy that I think has only arisen
over the last twenty years or so: it is this notion of two traditions.
Are there two traditions in Ulster? To put it bluntly, is Irish
traditional music 'Catholic' music? There is a lovely comment I
heard here in Fermanagh once, when a Catholic man sang me a
very old and bitter sectarian song, and his friend said, 'That's a
right toe-tapper!' The song had quite a slow melody, and I said,
'What do you mean: a "toe-tapper"?' and his friend said, 'It's a
song that you begin singing, and your friend recognises that
you're in 'mixed' company and he taps on your toe, and you say,
"I've forgotten the words of the song, I'll sing something else."'
This is a very good example of how people who have to live
together, who are neighbours, who have to *ceili* together, who have
to work together, and even though there is no question that they
will never cross a political boundary (they'll march on separate
days), they still have to maintain neighbourliness. Especially among
musicians, 'No party songs!' is rule number one.

Are there two traditions in Ulster? There is only one tradition
musically speaking, and that one tradition would cover the whole
of Ireland; but it would also cover most of Britain, most of Scotland except for the Outer Hebrides (where the melodic structures
are totally different), and a huge area of North America. If there is
more than one tradition, then there are thousands, because just
like accents and just like regional dialects, each area has its own
quite distinct style and flavour. If an Antrim fiddler is playing 'Miss
McLeod's Reel', there is no way of telling if he is a Catholic or a
Protestant: 'Miss McLeod's Reel' has absolutely no political position on the border, no position on contraception, on abortion, or
anything at all like that. Music is simply music.

Unfortunately, this notion has arisen. I think it has come mainly from the creators of ideologies who are generally urban people, who generally would be described sociologically as being 'intellectuals', and who have no direct contact with rural life. But you often hear people talk about – and I heard this from Loyalist sources – all traditional music being 'Catholic' music, and that, 'The only music *we* have is the fife and the lambeg drum.' Even *that* music isn't unique, isn't without connections beyond its own context and its own idiom. Most of the fife-players are also themselves fiddlers, and most of the fife tunes are actually jig tunes with a changed tempo. The jig tempo, ... , is simply changed to a march tempo, ... , without the melody altering. Many years ago the Hibernians marched and used many of the same tunes themselves. We have stories of drums being 'converted', as one man in Cullybackey called it, and we have a wonderful collection of old fife tunes in manuscript from the early 1920s from Cullybackey; and included in that is 'O'Donnell Abu' and 'Kelly: the Boy From Killane'. So, if they got a good tune they simply used it.

So, to finish up now and bring some other speakers into the debate, I want to tell a wee story, once again from around Fermanagh. I was talking to an old musician, and as usual in the life of oral tradition it is the speech and the crack that's paramount. You don't just say something, you tell a story about it, so I'll try to end up with a story like that, the way they did. This man was talking about an old neighbour of his who was a great man for sayings and wee 'spakes', and he said he was walking along this field one day and these strange apparitions were coming up towards him (they were pot-holers who were lost), and he stopped them. He was amazed by them, and he said, 'Where are you boys from?' He was chatting to them, and the man I was talking to said that he asked them every question in the book until eventually he asked them the question he'd really wanted to ask them: 'What religion would you boys be?' And they said, 'We're from Wales', and he said, 'But what religion are you?' They said, 'We don't really bother at all. We're nothing', and he says, 'You have no religion at all? Isn't it well for you boys that *you can go anywhere!*'

Lastly, to quote the great, late, and much-lamented ethnomusicologist, John Blacking: he used to define music as 'socially organised sound', and he used to say that 'a proper understanding of this music might produce a soundly organised society.'

PIERS HELLAWELL

Classical Musician

Sean's excellent introduction has opened up so many possible areas in which we could comment, so perhaps it's suitable that I follow on, in as much as he has referred, once or twice, to fairly obvious differences between the areas of music that we are here to talk about and discuss. We can look at the classical European elite concert tradition. One thing that I agree whole-heartedly about with Sean, is that some of the oppositions and categorisations which we are now so familiar with are relatively new phenomena. This idea of the 'folk-song', a term coined around 1870 as Sean told us, made me think of the same kind of splitting that happened in Western classical music in the same way. For example, in the late eighteenth century the pop music of the time would have been what was exported from the concert hall to the street, so that in Salzburg or Vienna the tune that would be whistled at bus stops and subways would be an aria from an opera that was actually being heard in the opera house, either by the landed gentry or the court classes, or in a more popular opera house where the working people were able to go and where the repertoire was very largely the same. And this distinction did not exist, and I think this is tremendously important because the social context in which we make music has changed enormously. It used to be entirely an elite thing.

I believe in terms of a more intellectually based music, in the sense that the monastery was a great base, and Sean mentioned this, and through the ages, we can see music moving around through different areas from which it derives its social and intellectual base. I think that this process is continuing at the minute, and this is something I want to talk about. Firstly, the categorisation of classical music, jazz, and traditional music has certainly taken place; and I suppose my presence here indicates that and shows there are signs of some kind of synthesis beginning to take place again, but it isn't a process that is going on at the moment.

I would just take slight exception to one thing that Sean said about this process, when he mentioned one kind of music being an elite kind of music, because I do think it is unfortunate if we say that of all the different kinds of music there are, people are going to mention one kind as being elite. I think this is true historically, and it is indisputable that in some areas of Western music, like those written for court dignitaries and court orchestras (such as Haydn symphonies), that these have their bases in an elite audience. I think that now it is very important to remember that the only kind of elitism is that imposed by the listeners themselves: if I refused to listen to some kind of music because of some social connotation, then it becomes elite for someone else. Obviously, I don't impose that kind of elitism on traditional music, which is why I am here, and I think Western art music is not the only one to have an elite: we all know traditional music has its own elite!

If I were to sit down at a session in the back room of a bar and try to play the fiddle, I think I would find that I was 'elite' there. Jazz, for example, is a highly socially developed form, and I think you have only to watch a jazz musician on stage to see that there is a real kind of social mechanism going on there. So, I think we all have our 'elites', but I think when it comes to listening, none of us does anymore. I hope not. I think we can all listen to different areas of music. Having said that, I still think there are misunderstandings and misconceptions between the unseen army I am thought to be representing, and the more traditional musicians. Two of these that have come to my note through consorting with some very excellent musicians, some of whom are here today, are to do with the whole basis of presenting the music in terms of writing it down and the way it is then performed. I do remember someone saying to me that he found it very strange that a classical singer could stand up and run off a string of arias from an opera, each of which presented a completely different emotional state, because one minute she was miserable (she had just been stabbed) and the next minute she had just got married: how could these successive masks be presented like that? Whereas, to a traditional musician, what was put forward was a natural expression of their emotional state at that time.

I accept the distinction, but I think that perhaps it shows an incomplete understanding of the aesthetic of concert music, which is certainly different, but I don't think it is based on dishonesty; I think it is just a different kind of projection. The very idea of writing music down is another area where I think we have misunderstood each other, and I think a lot of traditional musicians feel that someone like me writes the piece down, writes the score and then sends it to the players, and that I have tried to fix it so that each performance will be the same as every other one; whereas we all know that every performance is going to be different, and that it is probably going to be for a different combination of instruments. In fact, there is no such thing as an exact notation of a classical piece, whether it's by me or by Mozart, and so it would not be possible for me to fix anything. Again, the players are always different: there may be different numbers involved with different abilities, and in all these ways the music is different. We do have a tradition of writing it down, but we're very aware that it is terribly difficult to write music down. I am constantly being confronted by the inexactitude of notation: how all these dots are instructions towards performers that I have never met, and yet I know it will come out different even with those same instructions. Those are the misconceptions I'm talking about, but having said that, I think times are changing.

Many of my colleagues, particularly of my generation, are enormously influenced by areas of what we are currently calling 'world music': the latest in a series of inadequate labels! I won't call it 'folk'; I won't call it 'traditional' because we all have traditions. It's a problem. Many people are finding an exit from modernism in classical music (music that is tremendously dense and complex, difficult to play, difficult to listen to, difficult to follow), exits from that kind of style through the freshness and direct quality of the more traditional languages of music, and this is tremendously important.

In Queen's University we have introductions to different world musics: Indian music, Indonesian, African, Irish for first-year students in their first term. The moment they go to Queen's to do music, this is something they are exposed to, and I think that this gives a brief indication of how important this is to us now. I would like to say that the barriers are not down, the only thing that keeps traditional styles of music out of our own lecture curriculum is really the pressure of time, because the more we embrace different styles (jazz, popular music) the more we find the timetable getting very congested, but we are tremendously sympathetic to this, and I think that in this way, as well, elitism has changed.

I want to talk next a little about my own personal response to the traditional music that I have been exposed to in the last nine years. I must say that the direction of my own work has been profoundly changed by the privilege of hearing players, many of whom will be here today, and learning about all the different musical values; and I just want to say a little about the most important of these to me and to illustrate some of the products of those in my own work.

I think if something comes to you when you really need a change, it can be a very powerful catalyst. I was very much at a dead end in my own musical language, feeling that I was writing the kind of thing that required me to conform to what a lot of my generation seemed to be doing, particularly in Britain; and at this point a number of traditional things in Ireland became very important to me. As we are going to be dealing in a lot of general concepts today, I think it is very easy to come out with platitudes. But I want to be a bit specific for a minute. The directness and impact that is absolutely crucial to any piece of music lasting three or four minutes, and played for an audience that is only half listening and half ordering drinks, is tremendously important to me; and I have never tried to imitate the materials of traditional music because that is a very difficult area that I don't want to open up just now.

I want to illustrate the kind of simplicity and directness that helped me. A door opened for me, away from perhaps an assumption of complexity. This is the opening of a very simple flute piece that I wrote to a seal, off the west coast of the island of Harris in the Western Isles. I was whistling to the seal, and then I remembered that seals are meant to enjoy music, which was demonstrated by the seal because it disappeared abruptly: but I then went and wrote the flute piece as a kind of art music substitute for my whistling on the rock. There are three pieces.

'Song of Farewell'

The next thing that was very important to me, and again I am being very technical, was that Irish music, in what I believe to be its proper context, is played as a unison tradition. In other words, everybody is playing something approximating to the same melody, whereas, of course, in many textures of Western concert music they are actually playing different roles assigned to them. I think that what is tremendously interesting to a classically trained musician is the fact that the heterophony results in a lot of people with different sounding instruments trying to play the same melody. Of course, you don't get the same melody but you do get lots of different angles on it; a wonderful kind of effect for which unison is not sufficient. This highlighted the complexity of Western classical music for me, in the sense that there is so much going on at once. Here is something I wrote very recently for a violin orchestra (and I have it here for violin piano). It will show you what I have been trying to do, again, without having people play more than one note at a time. It might be up an octave, down three octaves, but if it is an A, it is still an A. This is violin piano, very briefly:

'Quadruple Elegy'

That was actually written as an elegy for the people massacred in Tbilisi in Georgia by Russian troops last year, so it has no Irish context. It's just the fact of its apparent simplicity of texture which is important to me. My last example is one which really builds on the energy, the rhythmic impact that any one of us will take away from a good session. It is Balinese. The piece is about the landscape of Easter Island in the Pacific, but the rhythmic thing is there, I think?

'Sound Carvings'

I believe the greatest tribute that one can pay to this or any other tradition is to leave it well alone. When it comes to borrowing, this can be a very generalised kind of 'burglary'.

Finally, I would just like to say something very briefly about the way we listen to traditions other than our own. Yesterday, Peter McNamee of Co-operation North used a very telling expression; he said something about being 'blind in both ears', and I think this is a very telling problem when we come to other traditions of music. At the same time, I am making a plea here for people who have grown up in the traditional area to listen to other styles: perhaps classical, avant-garde classical, or call it what you will. I am going to be calling my area of music 'concert music'. One thing I find foreign to the Irish traditional is the concert format, where *we* are up here and *you* are down there; and that is the traditional way of presenting classical music. I think, if we are looking for a difference, that might be it, although that is a social thing. One area in which I feel that I have benefited sufficiently from listening to traditional music concerns the rather difficult question of accompaniment: providing harmonic accompaniment to traditional melody.

A lot of people who come to listen to traditional music, from Western, classical, or pop, find it very difficult when they are listening to what I regard as the pure strain because there is no chordal accompaniment based on classical harmony. I think this is very interesting. The thing is, if you are trained in Western harmony, then when you hear these chordal accompaniments you know enough to know that they usually don't work; and this is because the music they are written to accompany doesn't necessarily have the same sonic structure. Sean talked about 'completed different modes', and I absolutely agree with that. I mean, anybody who has tried to harmonise Carolan's Concerto with well-behaved classical harmonies: it really cannot be done satisfactorily! I think everything follows from that. If people approach it from a classical tradition, often they are actually still trying to make the traditional music into some kind of classical music of theirs, and it's only when they let go of that and listen to something that doesn't need any accompaniment that they're really hearing the music as opposed to hearing, as Sean said, something quite different. I mean, when I came down here in the car this morning I listened entirely to electric blues from start to finish, and at the time I thought, 'This is terrible! I am listening to Buddy Guy and Eric Clapton; how am I going to "change ears" in time to listen to traditional music?' But I knew at the time that when the first reel starts and the foot starts to tap, that it will envelope me; so, I think it is very important to be able to 'change ears' from one musical situation to another. I would appeal to people to hear any kind of music, and that includes this kind of music or symphony concerts, on their terms and as little as possible on the terms of our own preconceptions.

Panel Chairperson
Thank you Piers. Something Piers said there is interesting: 'the escape from the density of post-modernism music, which is hard to listen to and hard to play', struck a chord. There's something I was told by a singer last week in Tyrone: he was talking about the wonderful sessions of the past, and there were people singing 'My Little Don', and he said that 'some of those songs are very hard to sing', and then he paused. Some of the singers are very hard to listen to, so perhaps they are escaping from the density of post-modernism as well?

DAVID BUSHE

Ulster Society

Listening to Sean talking about traditional music and handing it down, I think that is one of the major things of the tradition I belong to, the people I belong to. Their music is handed down and is very interesting. I would listen to Irish traditional music, also to Scottish traditional music, and I find myself tapping along, joining in the songs, and one thing and another, but what really stirs my blood is our own music: Ulster Orange music. I think that is the difference. It is the music of the people. It's what stirs your heart; and that's what seems to be left out a bit today. It's what moves you! Now, I was listening to very nice music there, but it did almost nothing for me. It didn't make me alive, and I feel that this is what binds people together and is the heart of traditional music, whether they be Orange, Green, whatever; it relates one person of the same group to another. I think that is the big part of traditional music, if not the major part of it.

TOM MUNNELLY

Collector of Traditional Songs

I am wearing two hats today: I speak for myself but I work for the Department of Irish Folklore as a collector of traditional songs, and I am also Chairman of the Irish Traditional Music Archive. The former is, certainly, the greatest collection of traditional lore in Europe, and the latter will have the greatest collection of Irish traditional music eventually. The amount of years I have been collecting songs was brought home to me quite clearly earlier on this year: I was in Roscommon, and when you are going looking for it, you don't ask people for traditional songs; certainly not for folk-songs. So then, in an area I wouldn't be familiar with, I usually go into pubs and ask around. There are old people in the area, and they have old songs.

Sean was talking about the collection of stick insects. For both the Department and the Archive, I think we could be described as going around with vacuum cleaners rather than with jars of butterflies. We can let posterity sort out what is 'traditional' and what is 'folk'. I have always been guided by the motto of the two German philologists, Jakob and Wilhelm Grimm (those of the fairy tales), and their motto was, 'The folk say'; so, I would see my role as being an observer of what the people are doing. I will observe and document; but it is not up to me, the Department, the Archive, to try to influence anything. To that end it is our role to absorb the information from the people, not to try to disseminate our idea of what is traditional to them. What continually annoys me are the conceptions people have. Fine traditional musicians, fine traditional singers, disappear up to Dublin to go on a tour. The next thing, you see them in knee breeches, green waistcoats and red petticoats! I think there is certainly an inferiority complex implicit in this sort of carry-on. It may be good theatre, but we are not talking about theatre.

I think that for Irish traditional music, Irish traditional song, there's enough in it to stand on its own: we don't have to sugar the pill. It's strong enough. One thing that worries me, and I have been collecting songs for a long time, is not that it is a particularly rare species of butterfly that we want to collect, but that it has survived for so long because essentially it is good entertainment. But we are losing the audience for the older ballads, and you can't just blame television and radio, although they have to a large extent taken the role of story-teller and damaged irreparably the role of the singer. There still are some pockets where traditional music survives in the home as a normal social outlet, but in relation to the older songs, the older ballads are being discriminated against. There is a form of sectarianism coming in which works against the dissemination of these particular types of song.

Nowadays if you are singing traditional songs you are perceived by a lot of people to be making a political statement, which of course is nonsense, but as we all know of organisations who promote this sort of attitude, people no longer feel confident with these older songs. They are not just perceived as being not good songs, not songs with a story; they are perceived as non-Irish! Now, traditional singers; they don't give a tuppenny damm (or used not to) where the songs come from. A good song was a good song: beginning, middle and end of story. But now if you are familiar with the story-telling tradition in Irish, you will know that a great deal of the wonder tales are populated by kings, queens, and by the aristocracy; and the aristocracy take a great part in the older ballads as well. There's a great example: at a house-warming, when I moved to Clare twelve years ago, a man was singing 'Lord Gregory' (you will be familiar with the song from Mrs Crone's single, or those of you who have read Joyce's *The Dead*), and I saw a very strange reaction to it. Another man jumped up and said, 'Eff Lord Gregory! What did he ever do for Ireland?' So, this is a form of sectarianism which has crept into song, certainly within my lifetime as a collector, and I think it is a great shame that these songs are being shoved to the back of the repertoires, the active repertoires of the people.

Here's another problem that I can put to you: those areas around Fermanagh, Sean was saying, where you still get the tradition of *ceili*-ing; whose music is it? What is traditional music? I think it is a fact that you do get a lot of performances that would be classified as concert, to the extent that they're done in pubs where there is a division of microphones and stages between everybody.

But as well as people getting out of the house, the radio and television, there is also the matter of affluence. People can move out more often, so that the social focus has switched to a large extent from the home to the pub, and this is not always a bad thing. It's just a changing social role, because those people that sing at home and who perform at home are very relaxed when they're among their peers; but musicians and singers (and any performers by their very nature) like to show off a little bit. I didn't used to perform in public whatsoever, but I certainly find that singers and musicians who I have recorded at home are grateful for the fact that they can be so relaxed. Very often they're missing that edge which they deliberately put on to impress their peers.

Now, with the matter of political divisions in songs: people now find offence with, or take a dislike to, particular genres which may have nothing inherently wrong with them. Political songs by their very nature, by the fact that they are expressing modes of thought which are shared by a group of people, by a community, will certainly popularly survive. And, just as an aside, in the Archive you will find all the songs which were generated by the World Cup this year. OK, some of them may eventually become traditional; they may be kept in a popular repertoire or they may disappear like snow in a ditch, but at least they can tell us what people were thinking, how they were acting, at a certain time. Both the Folklore Department and the Irish Traditional Music Archive try to collect whatever political songbooks there may be, from whatever side. I don't know if things will ever turn out to be quite as lucky as the night of the burning of the books in Germany; but in the Vostly Arcarde in Freiburg, they are very lucky that when the storm-troopers went in to burn down the library they found a large collection of nazi songbooks. They felt 'here are an enlightened people, so leave them alone', and that's why the German Folklore Archives exist!

I would disagree with Sean, if I understand him correctly, that 'folk' is a 'passive transmitter' of folk-songs, because you will find people who are conscious of being performing artists (people like Joe Heaney are very conscious of their art), and the dividing line between traditional and classical music can become blurred. I have only had the experience of being at an opera once. It was in Italy, in Bari, and, you know, when the tenor went for his high C, he blew it, which was like Packy Bonner letting in that goal in Romania. The actual reaction! There were cheers, catcalls, cushion-covers were thrown at the tenor, so he had to take another run at it, and he got it this time, to great applause. So, you can get folk reactions to everything. By virtue of the fact that so many people in Wales have such a strong choral tradition, are these people not 'folk'? The whole area is so blurred. I will just finish off by saying that, as far as I am concerned, Irish traditional music and traditional song is one very large jewel with a great deal of very interesting facets making up a great whole; and if one area of that becomes blurred the jewel is diminished by its lack.

PANEL TWO

AN ISLAND EXPERIENCE

Panel Chairperson: Sean Corcoran

Panel Members: Flora MacNeil
                Scots Gaelic Singer

                Mary Jane Campbell
                Scots Gaelic Singer

General Discussion

FLORA MacNEIL

Scots Gaelic Singer

I was very fortunate to have been born in Barra, and born into the family that I had. I learnt a lot of songs from my mother and her sister, from cousins of hers, and from a lot of other people on the island. I was hearing these songs from a very young age. I didn't really go all out to learn them; I 'soaked them up'. I was surrounded by songs all the time. My mother would sing any time, and I had an aunt Mary who would sing at the drop of a hat. She was a very busy woman: she had two cows, chickens, and all her work, but she would still stop and sing.

I knew Calum MacClean and Seamus Ennis who went to Barra in 1946. I was very young, and I went round about the north of the island with them, just a few miles. People didn't have cars, not very many cars anyway, so I got a chance of hearing these people in the north end of the island who sang slightly differently to the way my mother's people sang (they were from the south of the island, and my mother's mother was born in Mingulay). The people left about 1912, so the people on Mingulay (my grandmother) . . . I don't know how they had the songs they had, but they were very old songs, songs you would never hear in Lewis or the Protestant islands. You'll hear a lot of new songs in the Protestant islands but not the very old ones, and no doubt the Protestant islands had these songs as well. I could sing a song from Skye, and nobody from Skye would have heard of it, but I heard them from mother: how they got them, where they came from, I don't know.

I remember Saturday and Sunday afternoons when some of these women would gather in our house (I was always hoping they would come to our house), but there was this old woman especially, Mary Johnston, and she would come on a Saturday and I would see her coming, and I was always hoping she was coming to our house, and I'd watch her; and if she didn't come to our house she would go to see another friend of my mother's. But, it was always nice when she came to our house because all the women came and all the songs happened in our house then. She was a most unusual person. She had been born in Mingulay, where I suppose there wouldn't be very much they could do there; all they could do would be to sing and sing, and they all had their favourite songs. The women would gather in the afternoon, or late afternoon into the early evening; and they would talk about things and then they would start singing. If they came to our house my mother would have to sing first, and she had her favourite song. I'll sing a wee bit of it. It is 'Wet is the Night', and it's a song in praise of the MacNeills of Barra and their seamanship.

SONG: '*Fluich An Oidche*' by Flora MacNeil

That was her song. That, of course, was a work song. Work songs were sung while shrinking the tweed, and if the tweed was very heavy, obviously it took longer to shrink, so the songs went on and on, and the themes changed because they would have to work at it for four hours. One woman would sing the verse and the rest would sing the chorus. Now, I am sure they must have been working in Ireland a long time ago too, but I've been asking about it and people say there was working, that it did happen, but you don't seem to have any songs that were sung especially for it. My aunt Mary's favourite would be:

SONG: '*Gure Mise Tha Fo Eislean*' by Flora MacNeil

Another one she would have sung was about a warrior who fought in the Montrose Wars. He fought many battles and won many battles, and he had an Irish army with him. However, he was eventually killed in Ireland, near Cork, but this is in praise of this wonderful warrior.

SONG: '*Alasdair Mhic.Cholla*' by Flora MacNeil

I am of course talking about my tradition and how it happened to me. I spoke about my aunt Mary, and really I listened more to the women than I did to the men, but I wish I had listened more to the men because my uncle had a lot of beautiful songs, and this one that I learnt from him (most of the verses are from him and the rest from my mother) is a song that was composed at Culloden, and it is a lament for William Chisholm who was killed. The song was composed by his wife. It is a very beautiful song, and very easy to sing because it is so descriptive, quite remarkable! She just praises him: his manliness, the shape of his broad shoulders, his wonderful legs, everything.

SONG: '*Mo Run Geal Og*' by Flora MacNeil

MARY JANE CAMPBELL

Scots Gaelic Singer

Well, Barra is a Catholic island, and as a generalisation it could be said that the Catholic islands were good at keeping the old songs alive; small, conservative, conserving the tradition. There was an Evangelical movement which came to Lewis around about the last half of the last century, and at that time there was an effort made to get rid of all secular music. There were bonfires; and there was a bonfire (where I live) of violins, fiddles, and instruments. There was an effort made at that time to clear it out completely, and just have religion and psalms as the only acceptable singing; but what seems to have happened is that they created a gap in the people's lives by getting rid of the old songs, and what has happened in the last one hundred years or so is that there's been an absolute flood of new songs in Lewis. People have composed new songs. There's a lot of songs about sailing (which is a job that a lot of people in Lewis did), about being homesick, being away sailing; and, in fact, there is a common experience here with Barra, because a lot of Barra people were sailors as well. There are no religious connotations about these songs at all: they are just songs about sailors away from home and wishing they were back home.

So, there was a great flood of new writing because of the destruction of the old songs. I think that in an island like Barra there is not the same need to produce new material. I was at a little session with an old man, and he sang a song. Somebody said, 'Where did you get that?', and he said, 'Oh, that's an old song. That was composed about 1920.' Well now, if you said that to someone in Barra, they would say, 'That was composed about 1620', or earlier.

With the religious thing, I should point out that if I was a strict adherent of the Free Church I wouldn't be sitting here today because it would be considered an unsuitable carry-on, not even if I sang a psalm! So, the strictest adherents to the Church do not go in for secular music: they would consider it to be vain, worldly, and

a bit of a waste of time. A few of the songs that mention the Church
would suggest that the Church, as well as being a very strong
influence, was also a social place. Everybody went to church, and
once the service was over there was a lot of social intercourse,
courtship, and walking home from church which took place, that
wasn't strictly religious. I'll sing a couple of verses of a song which
mentions that, and it is a love-song.

SONG: by Mary Jane Campbell

The Church is mentioned, and what he says is that he goes to
church but can scarcely read the Bible for thinking about the girl.
There is another love-song written by a woman, and again men-
tioning that when she goes to the church she sees other people's
wives: how happy some are, and so on.

SONG: by Mary Jane Campbell

There is that same song about the manse, the minister's house;
and there is a lot of activity around the manse, especially for the
orduighean, which is Gaelic for communion, because a lot of people went from one parish to the next for the *orduighean*. It doesn't
happen so much nowadays because of cars, but before cars people
made a career out of it. They would follow the *orduighean*, and
stayed with people for the week of the *orduighean*, and then they
would move to the next village for the *orduighean* there. It was
quite a good way of seeing the place, seeing people, and living on
the cheap. There was one very famous man, Ian Daly, and he was
visiting in Bach at the *orduighean*, and the son of his hostess – it was
usually the old women, and even now they seem to be the back-
bone of the Church: I sometimes feel, if the women left the
Church there wouldn't be a Church – but he was staying with some
woman, and the son of the house was doing the taxi-ing back and
forward to the church, and he came down to breakfast and this
man, Ian Daly, was sitting at the table wearing his shirt, and he
thought, 'There is my good shirt he's obviously borrowed from the
drawer!' This man was quite famous, for God will provide all.
   Another song is from the Ness area, and it is about a man who
left Ness to go to Canada to the forest: there was a recruitment
drive to get people to go to work in the Forestry. He was sixty-three
when he emigrated. His sons had gone before, and they told him
to come on out, that he'd get a job and that he'd enjoy it. His

brother thought he was mad to go and live in another country, and one of the verses mentions, in particular, the chance he was taking in leaving the Church he grew up in, and he said, [initially quoted in Gaelic and followed by the English translation] 'You were where you would hear words from somebody who wouldn't conceal the truth, and today you are among wild tribes who haven't heard about religion from their ancestors.' So, he thought he was taking a bit of a chance.

SONG: by Mary Jane Campbell

The only other thing I was going to mention is that there are a lot of new hymns being written in Gaelic, and it seems to me that they are all written to old tunes, to Gaelic song tunes; and it's as if the people wanted to sing the songs but weren't allowed to sing the old words, so they put new words to the songs. In a way, most of the tunes they have chosen are love-songs.

SONG: by Mary Jane Campbell

GENERAL DISCUSSION

Ciarán Mac Mathúna, RTE
The new songs were very often songs from exile; people who were away from home in foreign parts, sailors, and they're in Gaelic. The funny thing here is that there are very few songs in Irish Gaelic about emigration. All the emigration songs are new, but 99 per cent of them are in English, so it is very interesting that you had songs of exile in the Gaelic language of people who had emigrated or gone away for years.

Flora MacNeil
There are a lot of people who left from Lewis and the southern isles around about the '30s. There are two very famous ships, the *Marlock* and the *Hector*, which went over to Canada. A lot of those people came back. You know, they tried their hand, but of course with the Depression and that, they didn't do as well as they'd hoped, and they came back.

Ciarán Mac Mathúna
It is interesting that the Irish-speakers who emigrated made up new songs in Irish about their exile, or the emigration theme; but there were hundreds and hundreds of emigration songs in English mostly, by the way, by people who'd never left their own parish. It just became a fashionable, literary exercise; but they wrote about exotic places when they had never been ten miles from their own home! We've thousands of emigration songs.

Flora MacNeil
Yes, I have heard lots of them. We have quite a lot of very good songs composed (very old songs) from the people who left at the end of the eighteenth and all through the nineteenth centuries. There was a very nice one about a man who had to go from Uist, from South Uist, where they put them on boats and sent them off

to Canada, and he left. When he was away he composed this song, in which he told us all kinds of stories about how wonderful Manitoba was going to be: but it was a terrible place! He wished he had the money and a suit of clothing to go back to Uist, but it ended up well because he did get back to Uist. His name was MacPhee.

Ciarán Mac Mathúna

The one song of exile in Gaelic, which is one of our most beautiful songs, was written in the eighteenth century by a man in County Limerick who was giving a lot of scandal. He was banished about three miles away from his own home, and he wrote this marvellous song '*Slan le Maigh*' ('Farewell to The Moy'). He was literally driven three miles away. He could have walked back; and only for the Priest who drove him out of this particular place we wouldn't have this beautiful song. He was back in about ten days!

Michael Longley, Arts Council of N.Ireland

Does your repertoire keep growing?

Flora MacNeil

There are very few old people left in my island now that have these songs. I learnt so many songs, so many around me all the time. I discovered people were getting interested in the old songs: they are a sort of folk-song, as they say, a folk-song revival; so people started to get interested in the traditional Gaelic song as well as the English song. I remember being in Edinburgh (I worked there for a few years), and as soon as people find out you sing at all, you're invited to a *ceili* because they are desperate to get folk to perform. So, I would go and I would sing some of my beautiful old songs, and they didn't want to hear them at all! People told me to sing something not too traditional; but they were the songs I knew. I knew the popular songs of the day as well, I just happened to be surrounded by the other stuff. I didn't feel inclined to sing them, and I just kept singing my own songs, but it took about twenty years before they were properly accepted. I am not saying that the popular song wasn't good, but I just loved what I knew. I have never refused a song, and I have given songs to groups, even Runrig have sung one of my songs. I have a daughter who is very keen on learning the songs, so I am very happy that she is interested in learning them.

Mary Jane Campbell
I suppose so many of these different old songs, from the poetry point of view, are hard to beat, because the actual words are beautiful and very strong; and you would be very hard-pressed to write a better song than the really old ones, and that's from the language point of view. I think that Flora would feel, if she was pressed, that the modern Lewis songs are a bit like pop-songs in Gaelic in a way, that they might not have the same lasting qualities as these; that a few of them might stand the test of time but a few may not.

Flora MacNeil
If a song that was composed in the twelfth century can still be sung, that is something! I am not against new songs, and I think that because we have had such a good, strong past and such good compositions in the past, that makes it good for the future. I think it is only right that we need to have people composing new stuff.

Mary Jane Campbell
The Evangelical movement is a thing like a faith mission. It would come, stay a few weeks, have big meetings like a Billy Graham kind of thing, and everybody gets very excited; then off they go and then things revert to normal. A few years later there's an awakening, and they would come back and the same thing goes. I don't want to give the impression that the entire Church is against Gaelic music, because that wouldn't be true. I think the most negative influence has come from outside the island: Evangelists from outside the island, from outside coming in. There are, for example, a few songs composed by ministers, things like love-songs, and they're generally on various topics about the island, etc. It is not a negative picture really, and the Church did a lot to keep the language strong, but they are starting to swither a bit now because they feel they aren't strong enough in their language and that they're losing their congregation by sticking to Gaelic. They are swithering now between going over to English, or not.

These psalms are an alien thing in a way, because they are from the south. Fife was a good breeding ground for psalms: Kilmarnock. When they came to Lewis they were changed. 'The Lord's my Shepherd' is how it would have gone, but once it has been changed, once it's been sung by a Gaelic congregation, it is hardly recognisable.

Morag MacLeod, School of Scottish Studies, Edinburgh
The thing they did in Lewis with the working songs was that they made up their own words, composed just for an occasion, but then someone would repeat them, and those words were kept; and then what I think were the superior words were forgotten. Barra and South Uist held on to the older texts, and I think that what Mary Siobhan and Flora have been saying about the tunes, is that somehow Lewis held on to the melodies, and this happened with the psalms they elaborated upon. The singing of Gaelic psalms is very similar to *sean-nós* singing: a lot of ornamentation. I think that melody is very strong in Lewis. There are other Protestant areas, you know; but I think they lacked melodies and they didn't take as much care with the words.

I would like to make the point that what Mary Siobhan has said about the Evangelical revival has been very significant in this respect, because a lot of the collections that have been made of good Gaelic songs have been made in South Uist and Barra, certainly in South Uist (which is a Catholic area, where people had moved from the north to the south, people who were Protestants). The main people who sang there were originally from Harris, the people called MacCrea; so the Protestant tradition was very strong at one time, but it disappeared more quickly. I think that is the way to see it. Certainly, I think that was the situation. Lewis people were keen on nicknames, so that the people's genealogies are very difficult to find, or will be eventually if this trend goes on. The original words of the songs are difficult to find because sometimes the comic words have taken over. Again, that is a generalisation, for there are some songs that have stayed.

Roy MacFaul, SEELB
You mentioned the songs of Lewis, and you sang them beautifully; and the songs of Barra which were also beautiful, but you mentioned that there are some songs that are common to both. Would it be possible to hear you both singing one of those songs together?

SONG: by Flora MacNeil and Mary Jane Campbell

PANEL THREE

THE TRADITIONAL MUSICIANS' PERSPECTIVE

Panel Chairperson: Paddy Glackin
                           Fiddle-player

Panel Members: Desi Wilkinson
                           Flute-player

                           Mairéad Ní Dhomhnaill
                           Singer in both English and Irish

                           Leslie Bingham
                           Flute-player

                           Richard Parkes
                           Scottish Bagpipes

General Discussion

PADDY GLACKIN: PANEL CHAIRPERSON

Fiddle-player

When I was listening to Sean's introductory speech this morning I heard all these definitions about traditional music, and I took fright very quickly because I don't think it is the sort of thing musicians concern themselves with. As regards definitions as to what sort of music they play, they just play it for the sake of it, and they do it. Listening to Sean's definition, it put me in mind of what the great Breandan Breathnach came up with when we were both trying to draw up a policy document for the Arts Council, back in about 1984. It was simply this: that traditional music is the music of the community, or region, which is involved in a process of oral transmission. Very straightforward and simple! If you were to take that definition together with the processes that Sean was talking about this morning, I would be immediately excluded from the whole thing, because the first conflict that I have found it difficult to reconcile is the whole urban-versus-rural thing.

I was born and reared in Dublin. My mother is from Dublin of Mayo extraction; my father is from Donegal, and a great enthusiast of music. Dublin at that time, back in the late '50s and early '60s, wasn't too receptive to the notion of traditional music, so how did I come to play traditional music? That's the question, and the straight answer is very simply, I was made to play it. It was my father's enthusiasm that won out in the end, because at the age of six I was given a fiddle for my birthday (I might have preferred something else, maybe), but I was told that I was going to learn this, and I was enrolled in the College of Music. So, I don't come from a background where there is all this spontaneity which we have just heard about from the Western Isles of Scotland, where the music is around quite naturally all the time. I was brought up in an area where there was no music around me; the only music being the few tunes my father played, and that was something I took for granted.

I was sent to the College of Music, spent about the first four years there; and really, it was a battle. There was absolutely no attraction for music in any shape or form. Basically, it was a chore, and you were learning all the usual finger exercises, doing Grade 1, 2 and 3, all those sort of exams. Even traditional music at that time was very hard for someone like me to relate to. There was no one around me, there was no one I could relate that music to except my father, and it wasn't until, I suppose, I was about twelve or thirteen that the first step in trying to gain access to the tabernacle of traditional music, if you like, was taken when I was brought to some sessions in Dublin, and I began to realise that I wasn't a freak of nature, that I wasn't somebody who lived in a place that nobody knew anything about, that was strange to everybody's ears; because that certainly was the perception that I had of it.

I began to meet other musicians of my own age, and it was really the human contact element of it that was so important to me, and looking back on it now I begin to see where this particular definition is beginning to take on some degree of relevance. But moving on from that, I was then brought into the music, again, in a sort of an artificial way because the only way musicians could meet in Dublin at that stage was in organised sessions by *Comhaltas*: the other sessions were organised in the old Church Street Club and the Pipers' Club. That's how musicians came together and swopped tunes. There was a certain social interaction, if you like. Yet, even at that stage there were still only about two or three of my generation who were actually playing: people like Neil Mulligan, people like Dermot Creakin. We would go along during our summer holidays, so you could say it was only for three months of the year; the rest of the year we were back at school, or it was too late for having you out at night so you were left at home. The whole thing was a bit of a chore.

The first significant meeting I had was the time I met John Doherty, the great Donegal fiddle-player. He was the first of the older generation of musicians who I made contact with on a human basis, in so far as he took an interest in the few tunes I was able to play (very badly), but the encouragement level was there nonetheless, and that always struck me as being a very important point. I was taken out of school for two days, and I travelled with Breandan Breathnach, John Kelly, and my father to Donegal; and I think it was the most important two days I spent in my life, in many ways more important than all the schooling, because it gave me an access to the real carrier of the tradition, and it was something I was to repeat once a year, sometimes twice a year, to go up and visit John Doherty and learn music from him. When all this was going on I appreciated that there was another force happening, and that was the more formal element of the music through *Comhaltas*. Indeed, I am very sorry that they aren't represented here today, because I would like to debate the competition system with them, where that awful word 'standard' is imposed on music: where, at the age of thirteen you went down to a competition (you'd learnt your three pieces and you played them off to perfection) where the people who adjudicated upon you didn't know what you were doing, couldn't play the instrument which you played, and yet they were up telling you what you were doing wrong! I always found that to be a bit of a contradiction, and I still do, in fact, because I think if you are going to impose standards you need people who have attained those standards, such as they are, to be able to talk about them and to adjudicate; and I don't think that has happened. I think it is a very serious problem which confronts traditional music nowadays.

We have heard the wonderful colour of Flora before us, and that is something that cannot be produced in competitions. Competitions, in some ways, can bring on a certain standard; but what standard? How often have we heard very good regional players going up in competition and not getting a look-in, getting adjudicated by people who know nothing about it; and as a result, I believe that competitions in many ways have contributed to the demise of regional styles of playing in some cases. I mean, how can you adjudicate between people like Denis Murphy and John Doherty, two wonderful players from two different parts of the country with their own way of expressing music? How any one individual man can get up and say that this particular man is better than the other! I thought that was a problem. I mean, I came through the process winning competitions, but they certainly gave me a false sense of my own importance, because really it has nothing to do with the interaction of music which is the most important thing. You were dealing with a product, and if you were particularly well psyched up and able to cope with pressure, that's what won the competitions in the end. It was really nothing to do with the interpretation of traditional music.

Another thing we encountered, coming from my particular

background, was the bigotry of music. There is a degree of bigotry in traditional music, and there was in particular around Dublin, because as someone who was attracted to the Northern style of playing I felt that a lot of the musicians around Dublin at that time weren't too receptive to it. I suppose they weren't exposed to it enough. To be quite honest, they didn't hear enough of it to understand it, and therefore when they were confronted with it (with other versions of tunes) they didn't know how to cope, and they therefore made the decision that it wasn't right. I'll always remember playing at a session one night, and I remember a certain singing musician saying to me, 'Where did you learn that?', and I said, 'I learnt it from John Doherty', and he said, 'Well, it's wrong!' That was very hard to come to grips with; but, thankfully, over the last ten to fifteen years I think people have accepted the music, the style of music of the North of Ireland, a lot more. That wasn't the case, I would say, until the early '70s, and that was something which there was a certain tension about all the time, and it is something which is now beginning to recede, thankfully!

There was also the elitism of music which we had to contend with, such as the traditional musician who would say to you, 'Classical musicians know nothing. They can't play unless they've got music in front of them.' That's a certain snobbery, if you like. And these were all the various things that went to make up the chemistry of traditional music. That's basically how I came to it. It wasn't the natural way. I said at the beginning that music wasn't all around me, that it was something that had to be worked at. It was a rural type of music, and being in the city you were sort of lost: there was nobody's door you could knock at and say, 'Come on and we'll have a tune', because you had to go out of your way to look for it, and that was a very hard thing to do.

Thankfully, because of a lot of different influences, traditional music is more accessible to everybody now. We can all meet each other much more easily. We can sit down and talk about it. There are a lot more things in print, which gives rise to discussion, and this sort of clears the way for people's minds to think about the music. I think that, by and large, we have a far healthier attitude to traditional music today. If that has been bought as the price for the demise of regional styles, then that's the way it is!

I feel very confident that the music which we are talking about today is going to thrive and prosper. There has been a huge development in terms of the numbers of players who are playing it. All that is required for those players to educate the ear is to be able to go and listen to the older players (because they won't always be around), and to try and learn from them and take from them the feeling of the music, the feeling for the warmth and the expression that is in it. That's the one thing that makes the whole thing so beautiful. That, basically, is the way I would come to it. I would be interested in hearing the other members of the panel here, because we are all from different areas: I am from the city, Mairéad here is from a smaller town, Richard is from a country area, and there's Leslie. Maybe Desi, you would start off and tell us about your experience.

DESI WILKINSON

Flute-player

It is appropriate that Paddy is from Dublin and I am from Belfast. Both my parents are from the country. I think that if you are a first-generation product of a rural background, you tend not to be a city person as such, and even though I am from Belfast, I have never felt that I was 100 per cent part of Belfast (probably because my parents are from Counties Armagh and Down). My first contact with traditional music, unlike Paddy, proved to be slightly lucky, because down the street from me, in Botanic Avenue, I had one of the best traditional musicians in Ireland living there. This was a man who comes from about ten miles down the road from this hotel, from a place called Derrylin, County Fermanagh: he is called Tom Gunn. I learnt my first tune from him when I was about thirteen, a tune called the 'The Pikemen's March' (also known as 'The Halting March'), and I found it a very attractive tune as a child.

I mean, at school I was going through the usual practice of learning music, which I really did find – and I would agree with Paddy – to be a chore. I was learning to play the recorder, and it didn't seem to have any relevance to me whatsoever, because I was listening to pop music, rock music; and suddenly down the street from me there was a man playing music, and it was great fun. He was playing music I wasn't too familiar with, but on hearing the odd wee bit from a song and a story that my father would come out with subsequently, even though he wasn't a musician himself, I could identify with what I was learning from Tommy because of what my father was doing, which was telling me a yarn in a certain way and singing a song. He wasn't a great singer: he was a terrible singer, and I am sure he won't mind if I say that, but I could get the same sentiment as I could from Tommy Gunn's fiddle-playing from my father's singing and my mother's odd step (the step of a dance that is). I learnt this from him, and I associated traditional music with people in a room; my earliest association with it.

I have since played it in many different contexts, as Paddy has: on concert platforms in foreign countries where people aren't aware of the context of the music tradition in this country, in pubs, in the most curious places and under the most curious conditions. I associated it first, I think, with people getting together, being very relaxed and very open; just great fun with a great feeling of general camaraderie, very vibrant music, and everyone sitting around in Gunn's kitchen. This was years ago, when I was fourteen or fifteen up until seventeen or eighteen. There wasn't much to do socially for a person of my age in Belfast. It was a very serious place. Often the lights would go out at eleven o'clock and they wouldn't go on again for maybe a week later (this particular period, I am sure people remember), but you used to have to creep around surreptitiously if you wanted to do anything socially, and usually when you went somewhere you had to stay there. It was very dodgy and frightening to go home. I was a great sprinter then because I used to run everywhere, and if anyone slowed up in a car I used to run twice as fast and cross the road.

So, all this had something to do with my learning traditional music. I know it seems like a tangential thing, but that is my experience of traditional music. I was lucky, I think, that I got the real thing fairly early in life, and I identified it with great fun and a great feeling: a great medium for human contact, and there was no show or ritual façade of setting people out and saying, 'And now we are going to have this wonderful person who is a genius.' There's just a man or woman singing or playing a tune: that was it. I think that human face of the music was the thing that attracted me to it, and I have been playing it ever since, and that's about it. That's my story of how I got involved in traditional music.

MAIRÉAD Ní DHOMHNAILL

Singer in both English and Irish

We were reared in Kells, County Meath. My father was from Ranafast in Donegal. My mother's father was from Cork and her mother was from Gortin, Sligo, so I suppose there was singing, and particularly from a very early age. My mother was a fine singer, but not in the traditional sense, and my father's family were steeped in singing and song. As he was a teacher, from June to September, Hallowe'en, Christmas, and Easter it was the road to Donegal. I am very lucky, I suppose, because I can remember my grandmother who was a lovely quiet singer, and we used to sit in the kitchen, the clock ticking, listening to the songs. Again, as a child I wasn't aware of what I was listening to, really.

We were talking about competitions. Coming back to living in Kells, the only opportunity we had to sing was at the local *Feiseanna*, and you had the youngsters coming down from Dublin, and you were put up there to do your bit. Again, it was a competition, and you learned a song and you sang it; and I suppose it was only in later years that we started getting involved, when my brothers and sisters starting playing instruments and we started to put a comple-ment to the old songs, which was something encouraged by my father. The Beatles were going at the time and there was popular music everywhere. We were probably more interested in that than doing something with the old songs, but all the same, you listened to the songs: they were going in somewhere. I mean, the memory: there is a great recall now in later years as to what I did hear and what I was aware of. Now I know what it was all about I feel at times that I wish I had taken in a lot more as a child than I did. When we were fourteen, fifteen, sixteen, we began to realise that the songs meant something, and we began to listen to them and tried to learn them. My granny by that stage had died, and my aunt began to sing the songs, and she realised at that stage of her life that she had something to pass on. She didn't think of it in any terms except that she wanted her family to learn these songs and to have them, and we realised that there was so much there, not only in the Irish singing, the Irish language songs, but the English songs as well. She had hundreds of songs, and bit by bit we became more and more interested.

You were talking earlier about the style of Donegal singing. The predominant singing was from Connemara. People thought in terms of *sean-nós*. They thought of the ornate style of Connemara and Kerry; Donegal singing was ignored. Maybe some people think it still is, but it is a totally different style of singing, not as ornate but beautiful in itself, and lots of people have commented that there were no big songs in Donegal: of course there were! It's just that they were sung in a different way, and sadly there are very few people singing them now.

LESLIE BINGHAM

Flute-player

I agree so much with what most people have said about traditional music this morning, from Sean Corcoran on. There is yourself [referring to Paddy Glackin], and you talked about coming up in the town and learning tunes; and I can see it in my own family. I can just see them play as you play it. In fact, there is a story going about our house: our daughter, as you know, plays the flute, and one time she was learning this particular tune and playing it a bit differently, and I said, 'Tara, you go to your room and don't come down until you get it right.' So, this has evolved down through the years, and Tara keeps saying that, 'My father used to send me to bed until I learnt a tune!' You know? She has two children of her own, and I am just waiting until she says, 'Danny, go to your room until you have your homework done!'

Music is a bit like that. You talked about the adjudication: absolutely correct! If you put me in front of Seamus Tansey and Desi Wilkinson, Cathal McConnell and dozens of flute-players, how could anyone pick from them? I agree, maybe it's good for children up to about eight or nine, for it gives them something to work for and it gives them a friendship. Our children are still meeting people who they competed with when they were young, as you made friends through it, you know? I'd like now to mention the whole thing that this conference is based on this weekend. I have a few comments to make on it.

Sean Corcoran said a great thing this morning: 'If someone plays a tune, you can't tell whether they're a Catholic or a Protestant.' Well, the first man that taught me was a flute-player called James McMahon. He is dead and gone, and his mate was a fiddle-player called Tommy Gunn (whom Desi was talking about earlier on), and I heard James and Tommy playing, and I didn't know whether they were Catholics or Protestants – and I didn't mind – and they didn't know whether I was a Catholic or a Protestant. I was taught tunes by those two men in particular, and it never entered my mind that I came from an Orange background and that they came from a Catholic background; it never entered my mind at all, because I enjoyed the music so much.

I remember that I bought my first flute from James (he worked in an off-licence at the time), a new ivory flute, and it was the talk of all the musicians: it was a rubbish flute for you couldn't have got a note out of it, but it looked good. He also had an old flute, and it wasn't much better, and I said to James, 'What are you doing with the old flute?' and he said, 'Selling it', and I said, 'Would you sell it to me?' He said, 'I would, I would!' I said, 'How much are you looking for it?' He said, 'I'll think it over. Come down to the off-licence on Tuesday.' So, I armed myself for that time, all the money I had, about £5 or £6, and I thought, 'I wonder if I have enough here?', and I went down, and James had the flute polished and everything, just sitting there, and I blew on it. I said, 'That's great James', and I thought, 'Have I enough here?' I said, 'How much James?' He said, 'I wouldn't like to lose on that flute. I paid a lot of money for that flute.' I thought, 'I can give him the rest later if I haven't enough', so I said, 'How much James?' He said, 'Well, it cost me 37s. 6d. in Kavanagh's.' I gave him £2 for it, and I still have that flute.

But, back to Catholics and Protestants. It didn't matter. There was a group I played with in Dublin at one time away in the early '60s, The McKennas: a mandolin-player, a guitar-player (Pat Stokes was a brother-in-law); and I never knew until about a year ago that they were Catholics. We have been playing all these years together from time to time, and it just doesn't come into the music. I heard a fellow on Downtown Radio the other night saying that only Catholics can play 'Catholic' music and Protestants 'Protestant' music: that's a lot of nonsense! I listened to Paddy Tunney in Omagh last week singing 'The Bold Orange Heroes of Comber' at the top of his voice!

RICHARD PARKES

Scottish Bagpipes

As a Scottish bagpiper I am at a great disadvantage, because when you meet people and they find out that you are a musician, they ask you what type of instrument you play. I think a lot has to do with the lack of exposure that both Scottish pipers and pipe bands in general have. There is a great crossover between traditional Irish music, traditional Scottish music, and pipe bands. A lot of the gigs, reels, hornpipes, airs, are also played by the leading traditional musicians of both countries, and if people would take the time to listen to some of the music Scottish pipers and pipe bands are playing I think they would really enjoy it. People really switch off when they see a Scottish piper taking his pipes out: you see kids putting their hands over their ears and people walking out, but there are people who stay to listen. I've played in quite a few of the folk clubs in and around Belfast, and indeed all over Northern Ireland. Some people say, 'Oh, no! Not the pipes!', but once I start to play they say, 'Oh, I didn't know you could play that tune on the pipes.' All of a sudden they start to relate to it and they get in to it. I guarantee that most people here haven't heard myself or any other top Scottish piper playing Irish tunes or tunes in an Irish style. How many people have? Not many people really. I think that when you do hear me play you'll be surprised.

Originally, I started playing the pipes through social reasons. I was at primary school, and a few of the boys were in a pipe band and my uncle was in a pipe band, and when my mother heard this I think she was glad to get myself and my brother out of the house for a night, or two nights, a week to go to the band and give them a bit of peace (my brother is a drummer). So, I eventually learnt to play the pipes. It was one night when I was listening to a programme on TV, when I was about twelve or thirteen (I was listening to the Chieftains), that I suddenly realised that one of the tunes they were playing was one of the tunes I played. I thought that was good, because I had no idea where that tune had come from. When we were being taught to play we got the music handed to us: we got no background information. We got the tune: 'You are playing the jig!' That was it. We had no idea where it came from, whether it was Irish, Scottish, American, or from New Zealand. So, when I heard this tune I got interested, and I started to listen to a bit more of this and I started to listen to other bands, the Bothy Band, and then I got a record of Paddy Kennan and I heard him play: it blew my mind. I couldn't believe how fast this guy's fingers could move: I didn't think people's fingers could move that fast, so that gave me a great incentive and I wanted to practise and to try to get my fingers to move at a similar pace to that, play similar tunes and get interested in this music. I think I have gone a little way to achieving that, and I have heard people playing Scottish pipes, believe it or not, who could move their fingers equally as fast; although, I think that is a talent which is given to you. You can never practise or train you fingers to move that fast, though you don't have to be able to move that fast in order to be able to play good music. That was how I got into the music.

The competition aspect of pipe bands is slightly different to what the other musicians have been saying. In the main, the adjudicators of pipe bands, or Scottish pipes, have been good exponents themselves at some time or another. At the top solo competitions in Scotland you have all the previous winners of various competitions judging at the competition, so you know that any criticism they give you, that they've been there themselves. They know what you are going through when you are on stage. I think that competitions for pipes and pipe bands are the only exposure pipers and pipe bands have because, apart from the competition, you would never see a pipe band playing (apart from the obvious parades and whatever). You would never see a pipe band playing on stage or playing and not moving, sitting down or whatever, standing in one position playing tunes, jigs, reels: you would never see it if it wasn't for the competitions. So, the competitions, in terms of pipers and pipe bands, have been a great incentive for the bands to practise and to get better, and go out on a Saturday and play.

Granted, sometimes the pressure you are put under playing in competitions means you can't perform as well and play the music as well as you could in a relaxed situation; but sometimes, basically, the people who win the competitions are, as Paddy said, the people who can control their nerves under those situations, and there are a lot of those people! For example, the number of pipe bands there are in Northern Ireland today is about 100 competing bands, all with an average of ten pipers each. So, you've got 1,000 competing pipers in Northern Ireland, and plenty of those people can hold their nerve when they are playing.

There has been a great trend over the last few years for some of the more modern and younger Scottish pipers to play traditional Irish music on the Scottish pipes. It is very difficult, and there are a lot of tunes which don't fit. The Scottish pipes don't have the range of notes: they only have nine notes, and they have one octave plus one note, and it is very difficult to arrange some of the tunes to fit the pipes. I have heard some tunes that have had a terrible job done on them, and it has actually ruined the tune! I am in favour of that kind of thing, providing the tune is still there and it hasn't had to be doctored too much in order to fit the pipes; and I think that a lot of composers are composing tunes in an Irish style, and this is a recent development. The fact that Irish music is now accepted on the Scottish pipes can be illustrated by the fact that at the top solo piping competition, which is the Northern meeting at Inverness, there is a jig competition, and a couple of years ago I won the jig competition playing an Irish jig! So, the top competition in Scotland was won by an Irishman playing an Irish tune. I think that must have been a first. There is a great acceptance of Irish music on the pipes.

I think it would be great if Scottish pipes could get more exposure through the media, or whatever, and I think if people would take the time to listen to the Scottish pipes they would enjoy the music, because there is a great crossover between the traditional Irish and the Scottish pipe music, which often seems to get left to the side on its own, but it really is an integral part of it.

GENERAL DISCUSSION

Dick Mac Gabhann, UU Magee
There seems to be an implicit reluctance, on the part of the
speakers who've commented to acknowledge the existence of an
urban tradition. You yourself [referring to Paddy Glackin] seemed
to be reluctant to acknowledge that. It seems somewhat surprising,
given that there are so many musicians now working and operat-
ing within an urban setting. Could I ask you directly: is there such
a thing as an urban tradition, and if there is, how would you
categorise it?

Paddy Glackin
There wasn't an urban tradition: that is the problem, and that was
the whole dilemma at the time. It was, basically, people from the
country happened to find themselves in Dublin, scattered all over
the city, and there was no particular place they could go to apart
from these organised sessions. I haven't acknowledged an urban
tradition because I wasn't aware of it at that time, even though
some of the best solo performers (on all instruments) happened
to be from Dublin: people like Seamus Ennis, people like Tommy
Potts, and these were musicians with a huge tradition behind
them; Dublin people born and bred.

   But in later years there has been an urban tradition. There are a
lot of younger musicians playing very good music, and they are
making their own of it. I find it very hard to put words on how you
would categorise or how you would explain the type of music they
play. The one fault that I would find with it is that there's a certain
sameness with the whole thing. It's very hard to distinguish a
player from Dublin as opposed to a player from Belfast, or whatever. People from urban situations like that tend to play the same,
and that is because they have been influenced by the same things,
like records. Pipers might tend to play the same two tunes together because they happen to like it, and that is fair enough, but

in terms of actually trying to find a style, I don't think that has evolved yet. I think it may come, but I don't think you could say there is a particular Dublin style, Belfast, or Cork Style.

If I could give one example of a player who comes from an urban setting and who has found his way right into the whole notion of traditional music and the whole concept and spirit of regional playing, and that's Dermot McLaughlin who is from Derry, but who has taken on board the Donegal style of playing very much so, and yet has still brought his own individuality to bear on it. He is a player who would, no doubt, be accepted by anybody in any part of the country as being a pure traditional musician with an identifiable style of playing, and a highly individual style as well. Then, there are people like Robby Hanna on pipes who would play with the best of them anywhere nowadays. So there are musicians who have done it.

Tony McAuley, BBC N.Ireland
It seems to me that what you are saying is that there are players who play in a regional style, but are there any regions or any regional players, because it seems to me that there aren't? If I was to identify the main areas of music I would immediately have to go to Dublin, Cork, Galway, Derry, Belfast. Do these places still exist where people like John Doherty can be found or is that now part of the past?

Paddy Glackin
There are people like Jimmy O'Grain; players with the pure tradition. They are still in Donegal: James Burn, Conn Cassidy, people like that, and these players are very accessible. They are keen to play with anybody who cares to spend the time and go up and listen to them. I find that sometimes in the cities, that there is sometimes too much playing and not enough talk. Most of the musicians, they sit down and there is no social interaction between them: they just sit down and blast music left, right, and centre, and it doesn't have any real meaning in any particular context. I believe there are areas all over the country where you can go and hear a particular style of playing and a particular repertoire of tunes that you won't hear in other parts.

Richard Parkes
Pipe bands were formed to be marching bands, and that's where the whole thing started and has progressed from. It just tends to

be the case that in all pipe bands, if you are Protestant you play in one pipe band and if you are not you play in another pipe band, and that is the way it is, basically; and that is a problem. It is one of the problems that we are faced with. It doesn't happen like that in Scotland. There is still this problem of not enough media exposure for pipe bands. It is a problem that pipe bands are one or the other here; although if it was the case that the bands were exposed on TV or the radio more, playing the type of tunes and the music that they play, it may help to break down some of those barriers in the long term.

Desi Wilkinson
I think music is a neutral thing in itself. It doesn't really say, 'I am this, that, or the other'. Here we are talking about the social context; we are not talking about music as such. I imagine that the core repertoire of traditional musicians and many Scottish bagpipers would be the same. A lot of the tunes and titles would be the same. As Richard was saying, perhaps most of the people involved in the Scottish bagpipe tradition here are from one section of the community (I am deliberately avoiding using the term 'two traditions'). Traditional music is found in places which would generally tend to be nationalist areas, although this is not always the case. What I feel you are saying is that the music *per se* is not nationalist, just as bagpipe music is not Protestant or Unionist.

We, in Ireland as a whole, geographically, are aware of traditional music. We are aware of a reel or a jig, even if we do not like it, or maybe not like it for political reasons: either you like it or you don't! I was lucky in Belfast. I think those conditions are more and more difficult to find. Traditional music is found in places like hotels, which do not suit. We have a problem in terms of venues; not only over the exclusivity of their location, but over the very construction of the buildings themselves. We don't always find places which suit the music, such as public *ceili* houses or stone castles. You usually end up playing beside the toilet in a big red lounge, but it can be grand (or desperate)! Nothing is ever ideal; arguably, it's just as well.

Tommy Fegan, Conference Chairperson
The social context isn't very conducive to Irish music throughout Ireland, North and South. The fact of the matter is that you cannot walk into a pub in Markethill or on the Shankill Road and have a real

chance of finding a traditional session, like you would have in other areas; and there is a big gap there to a certain degree.

Desi Wilkinson
I think that is up to the people at the end of the day. You can only say the music is *not* making a political statement: you can only say that. After that it is up to the people of Markethill, for instance, to start playing it and to begin playing in pubs; in short, to feel comfortable with it.

Piers Hellawell, Queen's University of Belfast
Ultimately, it is up to the people to go and listen to what they want. I think this is a problem in all kinds of music: look at jazz. Every kind of music has its established venues. Leaving aside the *us* and *them* you were talking about, it's a different kind of thing when it comes to classical audiences. I think part of the reason is that we can get most of our music through the radio, discs, records, and through tapes. Therefore, we do not make the effort that Desi has just referred to. I remember a very lively discussion on Radio Ulster a few years ago which centred on people going to hear the Ulster Orchestra at the Opera House, and 'what was the Arts Council's money going on?' A well-known gentleman from West Belfast was grumbling about tickets for the Ulster Orchestra. He never admitted that he had never been, but admitted that tickets must have been very expensive; and going down the Falls Road on the bus someone from the orchestra pointed out that it was only a quarter of a mile on the bus and that you could get in for £2. Basically, this was a problem of perception: people would think that this was not for them due to a whole lot of reasons. The only reason that I hear lots of traditional music is that I do not always know where I am when I go to hear it.

Desi Wilkinson
I *do* think that the question of the social context of the music is very relevant. There's a difficulty about where it is played and putting it in the right context, and that could have a lot to do with why it is not perceived as acceptable.

Piers Hellawell
We found that trying to mix different languages of music in events is not so easy; for example, classical music in Queen's and a jazz

event. If the jazz event is in the Dunbar (which is on the other side of town), it is a different crowd of people; and in the past we've found that it's very hard to get people to go from one to the other, because it really is a matter of getting up and going. Apart from that, it is a matter of getting up and going from one type of event, where you're sitting in your numbered seat and clapping, to go into a different kind of event where there are drinks and people talking in the background. That is a different thing to do in the one evening, and it's a curious type of social change. I think we have to accept that music brings these things with it.

John Walker, Central Community Relations Unit, Stormont
I think the point that Tommy Fegan made is absolutely central to this conference. The fact is: classical music and jazz do not lead to social division, to community division and strife, which I think traditional music does; and I don't think the problem lies amongst the people who participate. Catholics and Protestants participate without any problems, but in the popular way that traditional Irish music is associated (in a broad popular way) with a Catholic population, that rules out a Protestant population; and I think it is a source of social division, and it is unfortunate that people feel uncomfortable. In a sense, this conference should be addressing issues that people do not feel comfortable talking about. If we cannot talk it out in a conference like this, where can we talk it out amongst Catholics and Protestants? There's a case for both sides to have more of a willingness to debate the issues, debate whose music it is, and debate it in a way which is promoting better understanding and not promoting division and strife.

Desi Wilkinson
In a way, I think it might be interesting, in view of what you said, to talk about these perceptions and where they came from.

Will Glendinning, N.Ireland Community Relations Council
I think it has to do with the trappings which come with the music, and not the music itself. It has got to do with how that music is going to be used by components of the political persuasions. I may be wrong with regards to this, but there was one time when a decision was made that you were not allowed to play traditional music or to dance any traditional dance in any hall were the traditional flag was flown or where 'The Queen' was played. That

occurred sometime in the '50s, which in fact was one of the things which stopped it occurring in Protestant halls where it had occurred before. There is, also, the way in which pipe music is used triumphantly by Orange bands and 'Kick-the-Pope' bands, etc.

I think that if we are discussing *whose* music it is, then we have got to work out ways in which music is available without the trappings so that everybody can enjoy it, and so that we do not have to have it always with a Union Jack or a tricolour stuck on to it. We held an event in a community centre recently, and everybody said that there was no problem about this community centre; but when you drove down the road there were things on the walls like 'Seamus Mallon is an Informer'. If you were a Protestant coming into the area and you saw these words; it's a bit off-putting, considering what your perception of Seamus Mallon is. It makes you feel a bit alien and a bit threatened in going to the place. That is something which I am trying to get across.

Paddy Glackin

That is something which I have encountered playing in the North: 'Where are we playing tonight?' and 'Is it OK to play there?' That's a question which we have to ask, but, fortunately, it's a question which you do not have to ask in the South: you could go anywhere to play. There are certain parts of Dublin where you wouldn't like to take the fiddle out, I guarantee you, because it would not be too welcome, and that would be because the music isn't welcome as such: it wouldn't be due to people making statements about it. Certainly, I also like to know where I am playing, especially in a place like Belfast.

Jim O'Hara, British Association for Irish Studies

I also think you need to put it in a historical background. If you go back to the period of the Elizabethan Conquest and to the Gaelic civilization; the bards, poets, and minstrels were associated with resistance to the conquest. After that it was the bards and poets, again, who represented a dying tradition, which was broadly identified with a nationalist tradition; and I think that hung on. There's still a throwback to that. It certainly continued into the eighteenth and nineteenth centuries, and was picked up again by the more popular melodies from people like Tom Moore, the Young Irelanders. Here is something which has continued right through to the twentieth century, and I think, even unconsciously, people tend to identify some of the music, and indeed some of the melodies, with that historical throwback.

Paddy Glackin

Perhaps it was unfortunate that the *Fleadh* was cancelled back in 1970 over solidarity with people in the North. I think that was something which was supposed to straddle both positions. In fairness, *Comhaltas* have said that they are more than just a music organisation. They've made that statement more than a few times; and they have got themselves involved in other issues which are quite irrelevant to music. There is not an awful lot that musicians can do about that if the powers that be in *Comhaltas* decide that they want to make statements, other than withdrawing membership and deciding that they no longer want to be part of the organisation.

PANEL FOUR

TRADITIONAL MUSIC: THE PUBLIC PERCEPTION

Panel Chairperson: Cathal Goan
Traditional Music Producer RTE

Panel Members: Tony McAuley
BBC N.Ireland TV Producer
and Folk-singer

Andy Crockart
Commissioning Editor for UTV

Ciarán Mac Mathúna
RTE Broadcaster and Collector
of Irish Folk Music

Dermot McLaughlin
Fiddle-player and Music Officer
with *An Chomhairle Ealaíon*

Riobard Mac Góráin
Founding Member of *Gael-Linn*

General Discussion

CATHAL GOAN

Traditional Music Producer, RTE

There were a couple of things mentioned in the last section which seem to be central to what we are talking about: what the music itself is, then the social context for that music. I would like, first of all, to deal with the social context of it from my own perspective. We are essentially talking about a music which is in the instrumental tradition and is not much more than about 200 years old. Tom Munnelly referred to older songs earlier on, and in the Irish language we are talking about songs which very often go a bit further back, but it is not an enormously ancient tradition in the strictest sense of the word. What we hear in traditional music is music that is common in country areas. It has, as Paddy Glackin said, uncomfortably arrived in the city, and it is a music which is largely unselfconscious: people picked up what they wanted to pick up. Most of the songs wouldn't have had any direct relevance to the subject of Catholics and Protestants; they were for the most part songs about lovers' trysts, and the strictly political type of song wouldn't constitute, I imagine, more than about 5 or 6 per cent of the repertoire of most singers who sing Irish music. As Sean Corcoran has already said, 'Miss Mcleod's' isn't a Protestant or Catholic reel.

For my own part, as a Belfast man, it seems to me that the most important thing, on an individual level, is to connect with that music. I remember as a small child imagining that you had to have a Southern accent to sing traditional songs, because I was largely listening to the radio: listening to the Dubliners and the Clancy Brothers, and it was once while listening to a BBC Schools radio programme (and I think Tony McAuley was one of the producers), a programme called *Today and Yesterday,* that I heard a song sung by Davy Hammond called 'The Ligoniel Trace Boy', and for the first time in my life I realised there was a song about the place that I lived in. This boy, celebrated in this song, pulled his horse up the street, right outside my front door; and it was an extraordinary sensation, a sense of discovery. I think I felt the same thing when I heard the singing of a man called Robert Cinnamon on disc. I belonged to that generation of people who came at it from the outside; and therefore, that tradition and its renewal, its revival, seems to me to have an inherent clash in it. The music, from its natural state in rural areas, suddenly became popularised through the radio, records, and television. In a sense, it became formalised in the way that Desi was talking about earlier on: it was removed onto concert stages. It became about performance in a remote sense rather than about people on an individual level, and maybe that's where some of the problems that we're talking about here arise, I don't know?

The music in the past, for the most part, has been an individual and a solo art, with people listening to each other in a certain context, and talking about songs, talking about tunes; in fact, in the Irish language song tradition there is quite often a very extensive story that goes with each song. In the telling of that story there is as much pleasure taken as there is with the singing of the song; so there is a communication implicit in all of these things: a social interaction which is lost on the concert stage, or in the pub lounge, or indeed on the television. It seems to me that the only medium which comfortably accommodates all this is the radio; in terms of bringing an access to traditional music, and also being comfortable with the performers talking about themselves: giving it a wider audience.

Earlier on Paddy Glackin mentioned this business of competition; he also mentioned that there is no language of criticism in traditional music, that there are no established aesthetics for the music, no uniform way of judging it: tradition itself only seems to give you one way of judging (if you go by the tales that are told about musicians), and that is that the person who plays the most tunes or sings the most songs is regarded as the best. There are innumerable stories about pipers who have it out all night, one tune after the other, and the guy who wins is the guy who goes out for a break, hears the lark singing outside and bases the tune on it, comes in, and the other fellow doesn't have it: therefore he wins. Thirty miles away from here in Teelin in County Donegal, Conal O'Cuinneagain, a local singer, won the competition with a neighbouring townland by running away to his own townland and waking up a woman in the middle of the night to learn a song from her, so that he could run back to the competition and sing it, and no one else would have it! That seems to me to be the only evidence of an aesthetic we have in the tradition itself. There are no words about value and judgement in performance common to everyone.

In terms of the media, the formalisation of music which is implicit in it successfully getting out to a wider stage, a world-wide stage, means that the immediacy of the performance becomes stultified. Perhaps you get groups who bring great energy to the music, but that intimacy which appeared to me, when I first heard these songs, to be a key to it; that disappears. In particular, the television doesn't capture it the same as the concert platform because there is a remoteness involved. If you are in a television studio you have to artificially (if it is an older traditional musician) encourage them into a situation which is outside their own ken; the things like these lights and cameras around: it isn't a particularly comfortable sensation for it impinges on performance. I think radio might be the only medium which might give you some medium for performance, for comfort.

I was just thinking about this the other day when I came across a reading, a short extract from a book written by a man who was a District Justice in Galway, a man called Sean MacGiollarnath. He tells a story about going along the road one day; and not unlike Wordsworth and his Solitary Reaper, he met a woman singing and he was arrested by the beauty of this singing, for he had never heard anything like this at all. When she saw him she stopped the song. He asked her to continue it but she said 'No', she wouldn't, she was too shy. He then went on to tell a story of how it was the custom of the women of that area to go into Galway the week before Christmas where they stayed in a particular house, Anton O'Feena's house, and all that night they would sing their songs and they would be singing to morning. And this particular woman, Brid Ni Honough, was in the house this night, and she was asked to sing a song by the man of the house, and she said very politely that she would love to sing a song but that it didn't suit her at that moment (that she couldn't get the song right for him at that moment); so they all had their tea and off they went to bed. Everyone was asleep, and Brid Ni Honough called Anton O'Feena and said, 'Anton, would you like to hear that song now?' He said he would, so she sang it then because it suited her. I think that's one of the things we should have in traditional music; that individualism, with the individual as centre of the music.

TONY McAULEY

BBC Northern Ireland TV Producer and Folk-singer

I will continue by moving the discussion into a different area. I would like to bring a little bit of focus to bear on why we are all here today, and that is to talk about the theme of 'Whose Music?'.

I find myself with a bit of a problem because I think that the music has got a problem. I think that Irish music has got itself into a mess not of its own making. I'll give you an example. Some fourteen years ago I decided that I'd like to make a series of television programmes for Irish music – a kind of platform series that would suit the North. (I am talking now from a Northern standpoint).

I decided first of all that I would make the series as accessible as possible, that I would not in any way make it political, and that I would try to make it slightly seductive. So I used an old title (which I wasn't perfectly happy with) and called it 'As I Roved Out'.

I used, whenever possible, singers and musicians from both sides of the proverbial Northern House. I don't like using here the terms 'both cultures' or 'both religions'. The series was into its sixth year when a small but significant event took place. We had a happy crew, we had a continuing and popular series. One night some of the studio crew decided they would play a little joke – and it was meant only to be a joke. They put up a list of performers on the caption stand and a leading caption. It read 'Taig Time with Tony' after an old Ulster Television programme called 'Teatime with Tommy'.

Now it wasn't meant to be hurtful and I didn't take it that way, but it gave me quite a shock and it made me sit back and it made me think about what they were really saying. Collectively, what I was being told (now it was never articulated and it wasn't meant to be said) but implicit in the phrase was an attitude to the music. It suggested or implied that 'This is *your* music, and this is Fenian music or Taig music or Catholic music.' I think that is unavoidable. I think it is something we have got to face up to in considering 'Whose Music?'.

There is another problem. (I only bring these points up briefly because I feel that it is up to you to develop the discussion along these lines). I was in Cookstown recently recording a programme and I was eating with some old family friends. I told them what I was doing and a woman said 'you're doing another of those diddly-dee programmes'. And there is problem number two. 'Diddly-dee.' This music, our music, is perceived as quaint, archaic, very folksy, but boring and a bit predictable – by people who should know better.

And problem three has to do with *Comhaltas*. I'm an ex-member of *Comhaltas*. I didn't leave because of any row or disagreement. It just happened that way.

Anyway, I think there's a problem there as well. The problem is that its image adds to the notion that this music is not only Irish, it is Catholic as well. Not only is it Catholic, it is also Irish, and this idea is reinforced by its identification and its association with its governing body – *Comhaltas*. And *Comhaltas* has its highest membership in areas that have an Irish/Catholic identity. So a quasi-religious ethos is perpetuated.

If we are going to progress at all, then certain problems have to be faced, and I would like to hear answers to these problems which I genuinely believe the music has – not of its own making. I face these problems every time I make an Irish music series in the North for a Northern audience.

Irish music has a lot of goodwill going for it and I saw some of that last week. I went to a session in the village of Crumlin, Co. Antrim. The emphasis that evening was on the tradition of Scottish dance music. An accordion players' night out if you like, and there was a lovely buzz about the place. But essentially, and I think I'm right in saying this, it was the music of the Protestant tradition – the music generally seen as being of that culture. Not very different, not a bit strange.

How do we amalgamate the two traditions and make all of this, *our* music, and not *whose music*?

ANDY CROCKART

Commissioning Editor for UTV

I never heard a traditional fiddle until I was sixteen, and I joined the BBC when I was about seventeen and a half. Then I joined Ulster Television, and I met Brian O'Donnell, and saw Brian's huge personality and his enormous enthusiasm for the music. I mean, Brian had no worries about the religious or political side. I think the only time I saw him hit anybody (and he was a very big man) was at a *Fleadh* once when somebody kept shouting something very rude and vulgar and political, and he simply hit him because it was stopping the music! But, Brian wasn't making a political statement by hitting him; he was just shutting him up. It was a simple matter.

Basically, Ulster Television started doing the music because Brian got on very well with our Chairman who thought it was a very good idea that we did the music, and we started doing it; and, really, our problems at that time were not so much *who* should be involved (because Brian would select them), but *how* to present it. That was the big problem. In those days we didn't have quite such sophisticated gear (as you had Tony). We didn't have an outside broadcast unit and we hadn't what is called 'separate sound'; in other words, if we came out and filmed on location (where people were most happy), we had to simply take the gear and do one take. We couldn't do other little shots of their hands or the old familiar shots. There were enormous problems with how we actually presented it, so it was artificially presented from the start. That didn't seem to stop the programmes from being accepted slightly wider than we felt, judging by the letters that people sent in, who I think wouldn't have gone out of their way to listen to the music, but they actually would listen to it on television because television had a slight cross-community relationship.

In Ulster Television you wear a couple of different pins on your lapel: the other one that I happened to have was Religion. Once, after a live religious programme, the man on the switchboard (who was getting a bit agitated) asked me, 'Do you want to speak to this person?' I said, 'No! It's religion tonight, bugger traditional music!' So he carried on. He said, 'Yes, yes. We put out all sorts of programmes . . . Yes, we put out programmes for everybody . . . Yes, we put out Protestant programmes. We put out Catholic programmes. We put out Jewish programmes, American programmes. We have got every sort of programme . . . Well, you shouldn't speak like that . . . ' and put the phone down. So, there were those early days. There was the problem with some people of communicating to them at all.

That insight into traditional music gave me an insight into a huge amount of things. It was difficult enough getting people to play and trying to create a reasonable atmosphere for them to feel comfortable in and happy with when there were all these difficulties; and it is absolutely right to say that television isn't the right medium for it. We found that it was much better if you went to the right places and got to know the people and didn't say, 'Right, we'll meet you at two o'clock and you'll be playing by three o'clock', but more like, 'We'll meet you the night before, and when we sober up around midday we'll go and have pint of Guinness, and then we'll put a few lights up.' By that time, the man who was putting the lights up was a friend anyway, the man that was on the camera was a friend as well; and so it was all part of an extended kitchen. If you are playing in the kitchen, the person who's putting on the tea and suddenly gets up to walk away is not being disrespectful; he is just the person who is putting on the kettle to make the tea: and so, the cameraman is the person who is on the camera, and that sort of thing. We got some quite reasonable stuff that has now become archival.

I want to make two points. One point is this: it seems that television and radio are really quite good for traditional music because they are a fairly intimate medium. In other words, you can watch a television set or listen to a radio, and if it's done well and unobtrusively shot, you enjoy it. That's why I enjoy Ciaran's programme so much on a Sunday morning. It is presented in such a way that it tells you something else about what's being done, but doesn't put the thing into 'best' or 'middling', like, 'This guy is going to be very good. He is from Glenarm. Here is somebody from Cork.' I always felt unhappy filming at *Fleadh*s, because the one thing that seemed to be so 'out' were the competitions. I mean, the competitions reduced me to those awful days, either in the BBC or at UTV, where we had auditions with the kids being dragged by the ears by their parents, and they were forced to sing something they didn't want to sing, and all that sort of thing. Everything else about the *Fleadh* seemed fine. We have got a lovely wee piece of film of Felix Doran and his son playing. And, the look on those two faces! The look of those two together seemed to me to be the point of this handing on of traditions.

I think the other thing that we can do – and should be doing but aren't – concerns the archival side of things; and that is to bear in mind that the things we're taking now are for, or could be used for, the future. Just before Brian O'Donnell died he persuaded the Company that we should get a crew every Saturday for about six months and go round and simply pick somebody and record him at length, not for a programme (because you tend to be looking at whether he is going to play a reel or a jig), but just to get him to play what he wants to play, and maybe poke him into a few favourites. Bring back at least an hour of the man, let him talk his heart out, see him with his mother and father, his wife or whatever, and then just put it away! Brian died, and the only person we did who is still alive was Conn Cassidy. We missed Eddie Butcher, we missed God knows how many other people, but Ulster Television has consciously archived.

I think the media can help with the breaking down of some of the simple barriers: people not wishing to even go into pubs, that sort of thing. I think it can break down the barriers so that people can see people and not need to know who they are. There are other problems of description and presentation which we will not go into; but the more it is heard (and the more it is heard well recorded), the more people are going to enjoy it. Certainly, I find that contrary to what Tony said, our crews, who were not awfully receptive in the very early days, that is twenty-five years ago, gradually became receptive to it, because they heard it and they got to know the people.

Tony McAuley
By the way, I am not saying that the crews are not very receptive, but what I was really saying was that at that period (and I think it is still there) in the community in the North of Ireland there was the problem of *whose* music? It is still seen as 'Taig', 'Fenian', 'Catholic', 'Irish', whatever. That is the problem, that is the myth, but it is

still there. I want to know how we can further this process, which I am very involved in, of making the music cross-community, and that is very pertinent to the North.

CIARÁN Mac MATHÚNA

RTE Broadcaster and Collector of Irish Folk Music

I think the nicest criticism I ever got was from a great friend of ours: Donal Foley of the *Irish Times* said it was the most marvellous programme on the radio because if he had chanced to waken on a Sunday morning just after eight o'clock, I could be guaranteed to put him back to sleep in two minutes flat, and that's a nice thing to have said of it.

I am inclined to take a Marxian view, and look at the incentives to promote this music and the pressures over the years against it. There were social pressures, as well as political, religious, and class distinctions. In my time, there was a very strong class element involved, when middle-class people laughed at this kind of music, when it was considered just good enough for the countryside, and when city people and the middle class didn't like or didn't want to know about this music. Back in the '50s and '60s, on a long dance late in the night they might have thrown in an Irish dance for a bit of a laugh, but that was all. Of course, there was also the religious aspect, and it didn't just work across the divide that we are talking about: Protestant and Catholic. Even within the latter there are so many stories in the folk tradition told about the way Irish music was frowned on by the priests, and how they tried to keep down this music.

In that lovely session before lunch, we heard from the Islands about the fiddles actually being burned; but we've had that here too, with the priests frowning and not promoting the Irish traditional music, and we have the stories of the crossroads dancing where one or two people had to be posted outside in case the parish priest would come along (and they would scatter). We'd get the odd folk tale told about the many situations where the priest came along suddenly, and the blind piper was playing, and all the people ran away and the poor piper is left there, and the priest catches him and says, 'What is going on here? Do you not know that this is the Sabbath day, I mean, did you ever hear of the Third Commandment?' and the piper said, 'If you hum a few bars of it maybe I would know it.' There are New York versions of that story told in saloons, but they wouldn't be suitable here.

In time, the music was taken over by political and national attitudes; but it wasn't always that way. We know, for instance, in the eighteenth century (and back before) there was no religious divide in the loyalty or in the cultivation of this traditional music. I know that Irish people dearly love a lord, but the lords were promoting this music. The Anglo-Irish Protestant lords were promoting this music in the big houses of the seventeenth and eighteenth centuries; and they had pipers, fiddle-players, harpers, and this was a common heritage amongst both sides of the religious divide. Of course, unfortunately, in later times a certain political movement took over the music. The Nationalists said 'this is our music, and you can't be a good Irish Nationalist, Irish Republican, unless you cultivate this music alone and discard every other music!' These attitudes have survived up to our own day, even with the Irish language (which, of course, did cross the whole country in olden days). I occasionally go into pubs in Dublin, and one time, out of the night, a young woman came in with a box collecting for what was really the Provisional IRA, and she came to me and said, 'You should be supporting us because you're an Irish-speaker', and then I turned to Irish and spoke to her, and she couldn't answer me! So, I mean, you call the bluff. But, people have taken over certain traditions because they suit their purposes, you know, and it wasn't always like that, and maybe the day will come when the change can happen again: we can go back to a much saner approach.

Traditional music has now become fashionable. The class thing has gone. In Dublin, especially, all the yuppies have gone into Irish traditional music, and it reminds me of the sort of attitude you find in a place like Australia, where up to about five years ago you didn't advertise or publicise the fact that your great-great-grandmother or your great-great-grandfather had been a convict. Now they all want to prove that their ancestors were convicts, and it is the same thing here. People are now boasting that their grandparents played Irish music.

I was thinking that I might go away a bit depressed from this discussion, because we are talking around a subject – and I've been at other occasions where this has happened – and 'does it make any difference what we say?' I know that Irish music is a common heritage, certainly the dance music, and of course we also have the song tradition which is a common heritage of love-songs. But mind you, I disagree on one point: we do have love-songs like the true-lovers' discussion (which is very much to do with religious divisions), but whether we can solve these problems – and let's be perfectly realistic about this – the common heritage of Irish music may help to solve our problems in a small way, but don't let us think that it is going to solve all our problems, or the deepest ones, but I think it may help. Radio and television are trying to do something, but not with that in mind. I mean, we put on programmes for entertainment, but we are not trying to prove anything.

I wouldn't like to go away depressed from here and back to Dublin and say, 'What did we prove? Did we prove anything, did we solve anything; are we here to solve anything?' I would like to go away with an optimistic note, but fashions change and times change, and maybe one day this music may contribute in some small way to the solution of the terrible problems we have in this divided island. I'll finish with one little story about the standards and the kind of norms of performance that you apply to this music. There was a competition one time in RTE for singers, and a questionnaire had to be answered for the Radio Eireann Singers. Applications were invited, and one of the tests concerned the range of a voice from top C down to lower D; and one man entered for this, and he read this, 'The Range of Voice', and he answered bravely and he said, 'Four hundred yards'!

DERMOT McLAUGHLIN

Fiddle-player and Music Officer with *An Chomhairle Ealaion*

It has been said here several times today that traditional music has a problem, or is suffering from problems: I wouldn't necessarily agree with that. I think the music is quite healthy, and from my own experience from playing for close on twenty years, the musicians themselves don't have any hang-ups or problems about what they are playing or why they play. There are no problems with social intercourse in the music scene: I can assure you of that! I would say that some of the problems of image are caused by a number of factors which we have to recognise, such as the influence of the media. We have people here from television, radio, and record companies. What I get, what you get, what the public gets (how their images are formed), depends entirely on what you can get on your TV screen, what you get on your radio, and what you buy in your record shop. From my own experience, and I have been living in Dublin for ten years, if I walk into a record shop and look at the Irish/Folk/Trad. section, very often that is a chamber of horrors which will contain everything from James Last to Willy Clancy, from a fife band to the Pope's visit to Ireland. Now, where do you start to dissect all that? There are all sorts of problems of perception.

In my work in the Arts Council I have even come across, what I could only describe as, a benign ignorance of what traditional music is. Very often you start off with the three Bs: beard, the *bodhran*, and then you can add the ballads; and people seem to think it stops and finishes there. They don't seem to think that what you get on your record or on your television programme actually comes from a source, which is why people lurk around all corners of the country playing music, staying up all night, and doing all the things you have heard about. Unfortunately, I think it is practically impossible to capture that and deliver it for public consumption. Another problem is the comment made about how difficult it is to gain access, not only because of the venues and where they are, but also because of the rather heavy luggage and burden of attitudes and opinions which are stuck onto music for all sorts of reasons. *Comhaltas Ceolteóirí Éireann* was mentioned. I deeply lament the fact that they aren't here to address some of the points made. I would also refer to the Irish dancing movement: Tom Munnelly referred to the dancers who dress up in the zoomorphic designs of the *Book of Kells*, but he neglected to mention the fact that they have a pernicious influence on the music itself as an art form, so it is always presented as something very Green, and I can understand why people switch off when they see it: believe me I do!

Traditional music is very often also erroneously linked with the Irish language, with Gaelic games, with this vision of a very whole-some Ireland which, outside of the romantic vision, has never existed (and I doubt if it can). There are all sorts of problems like that. There are a few other things we haven't mentioned: the male/female aspect. If you look at the assembled company here, you would be forgiven for thinking that traditional music is for men: it is not! If you look at the amount of people of my genera-tion [late twenties] there is a fairly even balance between male and female performers, and also between males and females who attend sessions. The age thing, the urban/rural thing, all that plays an important part, religion as well. As I said earlier on, religion has never entered into my dealings, or into any of my colleagues' dealings in the area of music; again, that is from the practitioners' point of view, but I fully accept that there is an image problem. How you go about addressing that? That's an-other day's work. Who should do it? Is it up to the television companies, is it up to the arts councils, is it up to community relations groups, is it up to community forces? Is it about educa-tion, and should the Department of Education do something, should schools be more involved? The list is endless.

I would love to hear someone from the floor who doesn't know anything specifically about traditional music telling me what they think of it, why they think that; because that is something we haven't heard yet. Everybody up here knows what they are talking about, and I think a lot of people down there know what we are talking about as well; but why do we not have 'Joe Public' here, as well as *CCE*?

RIOBARD Mac GÓRÁIN

Founding Member of *Gael-Linn*

When I got the invitation, my understanding was that one shouldn't come with a set piece of any kind, that we were coming to explore and to respond to one another, and gradually to try to make our way. If I might refer to a point that Ciaran made: 'What are we hoping to achieve out of the weekend?' I wouldn't expect to achieve anything very solid or definite out of a weekend like this. I think that before one can change things at all one must have an approach. We can search for an approach and find out who else shares that approach.

I am not totally unfamiliar with the scene here because all my father's people come from County Down, a little place called Drumsnad which is quite close to Drumaness which is beside Ballynahinch, and on my mother's side all my family come from Glenavy beside Lough Neagh; two quite different districts. In my father's time, in his youth, Drumsnad was very close to being like the *Gaeltacht* areas that I came to know later on; full of song, full of people gathering together in houses and singing, and my father was a person who sang all the time, all the time! He had so many songs: that was his way. He sang even when he was driving the car. It wasn't a question of singing while he was shaving, he just sang out of sheer joy, so that was what we were familiar with. All his family would have sung, and many of the songs of that area I have heard since coming up in Mairéad Ní Dhomhnaill's area. Mairead Ní Dhomhnaill's aunt, from whom she got many of her songs, sings a slightly different version of some of the songs that were sung in Drumsnad, which I heard my father sing.

On my mother's side, that particular part of Glenavy was not a great music area, but as a child I happened to know someone that Cathal referred to, Robert Cinnamon. He wasn't respected in the area at the time. He was known as one of the old ballad singers, and accordingly (sadly, I only heard him heard sing once or twice) it wasn't for a child to ask a senior, 'You wouldn't sing some more songs?' So, I regret this now, and I didn't realise it at the time, but that's the way it was seen. He was a very gentle person, a very dignified person, and I knew him quite well at that time.

Cathal has mentioned the organisation he belonged to, and we were involved in records, festivals for youth, and so on. From the time we began, it was always our approach that we would respect all the people in this island and disregard any symbols that might divide people: that was our approach at all times. When we issued our first records there were six 78s, and we made sure of the fact there was one Antrim and Down fiddler on those records. That was right! That was the way we headed, and we tried to adhere to that as well as we could from then on.

We were involved, quite considerably, in entertainment occasions in the North up to about 1969, when it became more difficult to continue; but we always made a point of trying to go to places that weren't labelled. We didn't want to be in the parish hall, a place that one would be expected to use. That doesn't make things easier for you, because people have habits: in all parts of any country people tend to go to certain places for their entertainment, and tend not to go to other places. That's a totally human thing, and it's not related to symbols or to political views at all. In fact, you are trying to work against the tide if you are trying to avoid being labelled. We have a festival which is the largest youth festival in this country, maybe one of the largest in Europe, and one of the things we did at the beginning (even though we are an organisation which uses Irish), we didn't insist that the young people who participated in it must have traditional music. It is totally open and free. We like the young people to be involved in traditional music, but if they want to sing or compose in modern music, that's OK. If they have modernised standard traditional music, we don't disregard them. We would probably be regarded as somewhat unorthodox by the more pure traditional people for that reason, but we felt that unless you give freedom you can't really move towards something new.

By 1963, television news dominated the scene. We couldn't keep up with them, so we had to withdraw from it. After we had started our newsreel, when the first July came up it was down on our list that we'd have to cover the Twelfth of July. People in the South are very familiar with the Twelfth of July now from television, but they weren't at that time, and it seemed to us that one couldn't have a newsreel without covering one of the main events of that particular week, so we covered the North. We brought up sound units so we would get the music. We wanted people to see this phenomenon and to see what the music was like, to see what kind of a day it was, what kind of a festival it was. The man who was actually distributing the newsreel for us was a little Scotsman called Roy McHugh. When that Friday morning came and he saw the newsreel at the preview in the cinema, he scuttered up to my office and said, 'We can't show this newsreel! We can't show this newsreel! It will cause trouble.' There were scenes of Union Jacks being waved all over the place. He was quite right, Union Jacks could have caused trouble in Dublin at that time: they wouldn't, I think, do so now. But he was very perturbed so I tried to calm him down, and I said, 'Roy, we can't have a newsreel, and not cover one of the main events.' Eventually he pressed me, and I said, 'Look Roy! I don't think there will be any trouble and I can assure you there won't be any trouble because, first of all, the audience is going to know that it is a newsreel; they know we aren't going to mislead them in any way. Number two, the commentary will be in Irish . . . Roy, the Irish language can carry the Union Jack.'

We want the symbols that we are involved with, if you can call them 'symbols', to be symbols that can open things out, that can defend you against the begrudgers who will interfere. That's really what I was trying to tell Roy on that particular occasion.

How can one try to begin to make some progress? I think, first of all, the Chieftains did a lot of good in Northern Ireland, and there was all the work of Cladagh Records (for whom I have great respect). We work in the same field, and I think it is important to have others working in the same field as yourself, and what they do complements what we're trying to do ourselves. I think that the Chieftains have done a lot on concert because, in a way, I think people of all kinds, of all views, and all thoughts, began to attend the Chieftains; and I have met many Loyalist friends who have enjoyed the Chieftains. It occurs to me that really what you need to do is get your music through to places where a broad range of people will hear it: that is linked, again, to the places where one can play. The Chieftains went into the largest halls, and people came along.

There is another aspect that I might mention: there was a time (I think Ciaran was referring to it earlier on) when interest in traditional music began to develop. Traditional musicians were not highly regarded by the yuppies (I think that's how he described them: the word didn't exist at that stage), and if one had suggested putting a Willie Clancy or a Johnny Doherty on *The Late Late Show*, one would have been laughed at because it would have appeared that they'd have no place in it. They wouldn't be laughed at today. What I am saying is this: it wasn't realised at that time that a good traditional musician was as great a musician in his own sphere as any of the famous classical, or other musicians anywhere. That is better realised now. Maybe it is not totally realised in the North, I can't say, but people will eventually respect an artist who is understood and respected for the great skills that he or she has in playing and in music. When Ciaran brings together a Mat Molloy and a Jimmy Galway, I think he is doing the sort of thing I am talking about in another way; that is, when you bring a great and recognised musician and another musician who may not be known in the same way together, then people see that these two musicians have skills, great skills, that they share certain things and that they can complement one another in certain things. This may be one of the ways in which one could think of making a little progress.

GENERAL DISCUSSION

John Chilvers, Corrymeela

I am an Englishman, and therefore I cannot rise to Dermot's challenge in suggesting how we might go forward from the pessimistic strand. One of the things we've been doing in Corrymeela is 'experimenting'. We held a cultural conference last May, and one of the methods we use is personal hospitality, personal encounter, and exploration. We have been endeavouring to develop exercises with relatively small groups in order to begin to discover the authenticity of the values in the other person's tradition; the things which the other person holds dear as being part of their culture within the area of music. If you put together the players of the *bodhran* and the lambeg drum and enable them, with others, to discover the craftsmanship in the playing, the artistry, the subtlety, and the rhythms, and you enable them to discover that kind of commonality; then strange things begin to happen in terms of the personal relationships that go on behind the scenes. It is then that people begin to see, not just the bloc threats, but they begin to see the merit of something which, perhaps through upbringing or taste, they'd been prevented from ever encountering. The same thing applies to other aspects of history and culture.

As well as the policy-makers' and pundits' kind of approach, which we have remarked upon and questioned during the course of this conference, I think there's a lot that could be done with personal encounter as a method of discovery, rather than imposing something, which so many of us have found is not the way forward.

Roy McFaul, SEELB

One of the panel asked for someone without a background in traditional music. I don't have a traditional music background, so one of the primary questions that occurs to me is 'What is the point of traditional music?' We had a speaker earlier on who talked about Orange music being the music that actually moves him, and I am sure on the other side that Nationalists would find that nationalist songs would move them; but for me the whole point of any kind of music is that it is there for people to enjoy. If people perceive music to belong to one section of the community, then the other section is being deprived of that enjoyment; and I think one of the things we need to think about is the exposure to all the community of all types of music.

My normal practice, for example, on the Twelfth of July is to listen to the bands and watch the parades, and to take my children along to listen to it. Now, I am actually a Catholic, and I feel quite strange watching the Twelfth of July parade, and then I say, 'Why should I feel strange? The music is there for people to listen to and for people to enjoy'. So, I do listen to it and I do enjoy it. I also listen to Irish traditional music and I also enjoy it: so why should we divide the music? It is there for everyone to enjoy. We must try to get rid of the perception that it belongs to one section of the community, or that any music belongs to one side of the community. If we don't then all we are doing is depriving ourselves of the enjoyment of what we consider to be someone else's music.

Riobard Mac Góráin

I mentioned a festival earlier on, and we hope to have more festivals, local festivals, in the North; and next year we will be holding one in Stranmillis College, and we will also be introducing a competition for marching bands. We are doing this in the hope that a wide range of schools will enter, and if they have Stranmillis as the location, well, that will certainly not be a deterrent to their coming there. In other words, the place is important. Some people are shy about going to certain places, and we have got to find ways of overcoming that; but this is one little step on our part, and I think we need more, many more steps in that direction.

Dermot McLaughlin

I wouldn't suggest that everyone here is going to enjoy traditional music any more than I enjoy taxidermy, stamp collecting, opera, or whatever, because some things I don't like, some things I don't understand, for example: I will never be a footballer because I would be massacred on the football field, but at the same time that wouldn't stop me watching it on TV or reading books on it, or buying videos of the game. Unfortunately, it isn't so easy to do that with traditional music. Irish traditional music, or whatever you want to call it, is very often a hit-or-miss thing as to how you come across it. Richard Parkes was talking about pipe bands earlier on. I mean, if I had not been working in the Arts Council in Dublin I would never have had the chance to get into the pipe band scene, to go and hear good pipe bands, hear good pipers and get to know them, talk to them and find out what makes them tick. It is the same thing that makes me tick when I stick a fiddle under my chin. You play music because you like it.

I wouldn't advocate traditional music as a panacea for all our ills by any means. It is not. It is going to exist (and it has existed for long enough) whether or not there is conflict, whether or not there is television, radio, State support, education systems, or record companies. It will stay there, and that is a fact of life. If organisations take it upon themselves to use it for whatever reason: for political reasons, for reasons of ego, that is really their business; and I really don't think that the musicians would swallow that themselves. I think you'd find that musicians would be very willing to share what they have, and if someone likes music and they say, 'Where can I hear that?', they'll tell you. It is a very open scene, and it always has been in my experience.

Roy McFaul

I think you are getting back to the point that I made. The music is there for people who want to listen to it, who want to play it, who want to dance to it, and it is open to everybody. I mean, it is not one section's music; it belongs to those people who want to listen to it, who want to dance to it, who want to play it; and we have got to convey that perception to people, rather than the perception that it belongs to one section of the community only. The best way we can do that is through the media, because the media, no matter how much we like to say it doesn't, the media quite often shapes the perceptions which we have, and in that it has a big responsibility.

Dermot McLaughlin

I would agree with that, but I wouldn't underestimate the influence of any of the large organisations, such as *Comhaltas*, who were mentioned earlier; and there is also that version of Irish culture (Irish music and Irish dance) portrayed by *Siamsa Tíre*, the National Folk Theatre, which is based in Tralee. It is a very complex question.

Ciarán Mac Mathúna
Over the last twenty years there have been certain songs and certain groups that I have not featured in my programmes. I don't care (and some of them have a lot of influence in the music world), because I do feel that they are pandering to activities that I do not agree with; and they are making money, to put it crudely, with records over dead bodies. I refuse to put on records that celebrate activities which seem awful to me. They are celebrating the wrong kind of thing on both sides of the divide. In that sense, we do have a censorship. I apply a censorship according to my own rule, and I don't apologise for it.

Tommy Fegan, Conference Chairperson
Is that a personal policy or is that an RTE policy?

Ciarán Mac Mathúna
I don't speak for RTE officially. There is no written rule and no list of songs which I know of that shouldn't be broadcast, but there is a guideline to the effect that you should not broadcast any material which is going to offend the sensibilities of people in this island, either politically or religiously. It is up to every producer to use his own discretion on these things. I am not trying to evade the question, but there is a policy in the sense that thirty to forty years ago you might have broadcast things which you would be reluctant to do today, because you would be adding to the troubles and problems of this country.

Tommy Fegan, Conference Chairperson
That raises an interesting question, and one which I hadn't actually thought about when we came to this conference: how are those guidelines drawn up, how often are they reviewed, and in what context are they reviewed (within the context of political development, such as the Anglo-Irish Agreement)? It raises a whole clatter of questions, and that might digress slightly from the field of music, but nonetheless it is relevant to it.

Cathal Goan
I think they are mostly drawn up on good taste. Most of it is rubbish: you wouldn't want to play it anyway! That's honestly! If you get a couple of guitars in tune, you're lucky. A large propor-

tion of the music which might often be viewed as coming under the traditional umbrella has very little to do with it at all. By and large, most of the stuff that is being put out now is rubbish. It has no merit on a musical level, or on a poetic level; so you have to exercise your aesthetic judgement and say, 'I am not going to play that', and that is the way it works.

Ciarán Mac Mathúna

May I just tell one anecdote, because one answer has it that there is always 'an Irish solution to an Irish problem'. The entertainment on the Twelfth of July has been mentioned; and coming through Cavan today I was reminded of some recording I was doing in Cavan many years ago. I was staying in a little hotel (it was really a guest house), and there was always one permanent guest there who was very much in the Orange Order, but he had been part of that household for years. Every year he produced the sash, and then went out and enjoyed himself for that great occasion, but one year the sash was becoming very frail, so he brought it to the housekeeper, his dear friend, and asked her to wash and clean the sash; but her religion gave her a crisis of conscience, and she refused. But then, she couldn't let him down, so she got over it and said, 'All right! I'll wash it but I won't iron it!'

Constance Short, Co-operation North

I don't think we are really dealing with what Tony is talking about. A lot of us do walk about on eggs, hoping that we won't offend when we're singing the songs or playing the music. I am not a traditional singer, but I do sing a song like most people in Ireland, and there are songs that I would be a wee bit worried about singing, that I wouldn't have thought about not singing a few years ago. People do refer to it as 'Taig' music, and yet I was brought up to think that Protestants in north Antrim play the music as well, that it was their music, and so on. Ciaran Carson, who unfortunately cannot be here today, told me a story: he was playing in Kerry or Cork, or somewhere, and someone said, 'Aren't you great to be playing our music.' I mean, just because he had a Northern accent! I am a bit frustrated here because nobody is actually dealing with this: is there no one here that wants to deal with it? There is no point in saying, 'Oh, you know, it is about venues', and, 'Maybe we can go to another venue.' I feel that what Tony has started hasn't been addressed.

Mary Holland, the *Irish Times*
I would like to make a couple of points. I think there is a slight tendency to believe that this is just an Irish problem. One only has to think of the fuss there was in England when the conductor suggested that if people were dying in the Gulf, it might not be appropriate to be playing 'Land of Hope and Glory' at the end of the Proms; and rather than accede to what seemed to me to be an admirable sensitivity on the part of the conductor, he was removed and not allowed to conduct the concert because the BBC was bowing to public feeling in England. I don't think that we ought to be too concerned about this being uniquely Irish. Of course, Tony put his finger on it when he said that the problem (because there is a situation of conflict here) was that the music is not neutral, and that it is an absolute cop out to pretend that it is. Music is not neutral in any situation. The reason that armies have bands is to whip the soldiers into war: it is not to provide them with light relaxation so that they can enjoy the music. It has a purpose, the music is martial. That is why it is used, and I think it is quite wrong to ignore that element in it.

I haven't got a solution for it. I don't think there will be a solution to it until the conflict is resolved and the music is made accessible to be enjoyed by both sides equally. I take the point that's been made here, that every effort must be made to make the music equally accessible and valued as highly, in some way, as the music of the Orange bands. I mean, I must say it gives me a terrific, if a somewhat shameful, kick when I go and hear them. I think there is a real problem that it is not neutral. I don't know if the answer to that is to censor it or to say the song shouldn't be sung. The thing that finally convinced me that there's no point in anyone talking about Articles 2 and 3 in the South was a long session of music I was at in west Cork. After that I thought, 'forget it!', forever really, because as the night went on it became quite clear that there are very strong emotions evoked by this music, and they are there.

Fintan Vallely, Flute-player and Songwriter
Firstly, I would like to say that I thought the term for the conference, 'Whose Music?', was a bit provocative. Is it North/South, Protestants/Catholics, or indeed, is it men/women, because the majority of people who appear playing in public are, in fact, men? The other thing is this: Sean Corcoran said to me, in relation to

this conference, that some old fellow from Fermanagh said, 'Why are they blaming us?', meaning 'Why are they blaming musicians?' In relation to what Tony said earlier on, I don't think traditional music has got itself into a mess. I don't think it is in a mess at all. I don't see why music should have to defend itself against all this, or that it should have to solve the political problems of this part of the country. It exists in parallel; it just exists at the same time that the problems are going on. It was probably revived from the movements which were sweeping America, the whole of Europe, in the '60s and '70s: the post-war revamping of the whole of European society.

Political problems are not unique to Irish music. There are several musics from Bulgaria; the one which we hear is Muslim music, which is sung by a minority of the. population, but the Bulgarian Government is keen to adopt it as *their* music, even though it is not their music specifically speaking! It is Muslim music which crosses political boundaries. So, I don't see why we should have to defend ourselves.

Also, I don't like the idea of mixing up the tradition of Orange music (which gives me a great lift I must say, and I appreciate why David Bushe said that the music turns him on; and that's grand). I don't see why we should have to mix them up. As I see it, the Orange music takes a fifth of its repertoire straight from (as far as I can decipher) Scottish songs and Scottish marches, Scottish reels and single reels, and all the rest are other types of tunes which are adopted to march time. These Scottish tunes are the only common ground for me. But I don't see why other things are grafted on, like having difficulty in getting to a particular pub where the music is played. That's a problem to do with the political situation here, not a problem to do with the musicians. The musicians will play wherever they happen to live and find it handy to convene. I've played music all over Scotland and England, and I am generally playing to Protestant audiences, almost totally Protestant audiences, and we are playing with Protestant musicians: religion doesn't matter. So, it is a political problem.

I would say that we do have some responsibility (being people who play the music); and in as far as most of the people I know, who play music, appear to be agnostics anyway, the question is whether they are 'Catholic' agnostics or 'Protestant' agnostics! I feel that we have a responsibility to make the music available to people who otherwise wouldn't hear it, and that means Catholics as well. My brother used to nearly kick the television in when *Bring Down the Lamp* came on first. He couldn't stand it, as indeed most of my school friends couldn't. When I was at school I used to hang my head in shame when the subject of traditional music was mentioned, because I was probably the only person in my age group in the town of Armagh playing traditional music at that particular point in time. There are other people out there who haven't heard it yet. The Pipers' Club in Armagh had a concert for the twentieth year of their existence a few years ago, and somebody came along and said, 'God! Isn't it great to see this sort of music in Armagh. We never knew it was here at all.' The Pipers' Club was going for twenty years! We had concerts in the city hall at least once or twice a year; sessions going on all the time. We even appeared on your programme, Andy! So, there is a whole other audience out there: and I am not just concerned on blaming it on Catholics, or whatever.

Tony McAuley

My point, just to reiterate it in case there should be any doubt about what I am saying, was that Irish music has got itself into a mess. What I am saying is this: the music has been dragged in through no fault of its own, and it has become marginalised, or if you like (I hate to say it), in some ways it has almost become politicised. It is seen mainly as the music of one side of the community in Northern Ireland, and I reinforce that by saying that the problem is reinforced by the fact that it is seen as diddle-dee music. Something came out of the word 'folk', meaning something 'common': it was not played by respectable people, and I think that that still hangs on to a larger extent in the North because of this problem of marginalisation. Thirdly, I was saying that this was compounded by some of the activities of *Comhaltas,* unintentionally, but nevertheless, all these factors were coming and they were dragging Irish traditional music into a very unhappy state; and I believe that that is so, and I think that if you look at where the music is normally played, whether it is Armagh or wherever, I don't think that you can really deny that, by and large, the music is played in areas visited or lived in by one section of the community. I am saying: that is tragic. It should not be, but I don't have an answer; and this must seem awfully earnest, but I was hoping that maybe somebody would offer something rather than reinforce my own sense of complexity.

Fintan Vallely
I don't think that it's the musicians' business to actually alter the
political history of the country. Jazz is a very popular music form in
Czechoslovakia, but it is a totally subversive form, and for years it
has been identified by the State as being anti-State; but that
doesn't mean that the jazz they play is bad! It doesn't mean that
the people are playing because it is anti-State: they play it because
they are hooked on it! I mean, I play music because I am hooked
on it and most people I know play music for that same reason;
most people may have personal politics, but the music has absolutely nothing to do with their politics.

Aodán Mac Póilin, ULTACH Trust
Your taste in music is usually the result of the environment you are
brought up in or because of a conscious decision. David said this
morning that he got the greatest kick out of the music that
belonged to him and his people. Now, there is obviously an ideological sub-text here; and the same ideological sub-text applies to
the Nationalist community. Very many Nationalists decide to like
Irish music because they regard it as their music, so they go for it.
I remember the great relief that I had myself when I found that
Irish music was not restricted to *The Waltons* programme. The
motivation for getting involved in Irish music is not just purely
aesthetic; it is quite frequently a matter of choice, and that choice
is very frequently an ideological choice. Irish music is nearly always
played in Nationalist areas, and it is hard to find a venue that is
neutral: there are historical reasons for that.

Two small points: the first point is that nationalist music didn't
stop being traditional at the turn of this century. There is a living
tradition of republican songs, and some of those songs are still
good whether you agree with the sentiments or not. The other
point is that the few Catholic pipe bands don't call them the
'Scottish pipes', they call them the 'war pipes'.

There is quite a strong constituency among Nationalists for Irish
music, and there is a dilemma between that support, which is
perfectly legitimate, and the urge that we are talking about here to
spread its attraction beyond those particular confines. We have
the same problem with the Irish language. There is a perfectly
good ideological reason, a political reason, for taking up the Irish
language, but support for the language shouldn't be confined to
those who support these particular ideologies. So, you end up in a

dilemma: most of the adherents belong to a particular political tradition, and you want to spread interest in the culture, but don't know how. It is very difficult.

John Walker, Central Community Relations Unit, Stormont

I think it is a cop out to say that it's not for traditional musicians to change politics: they are part of society here. They are part of the problem, they are part of the solution. What I've found very positive about this conference are a couple of comments that I think point the way forward: Ciarán Mac Mathúna, I think you hit on it when you said that if we leave this conference with people saying, 'Yes, traditional musicians do have a contribution to make to addressing the divisions in this society', that I think is a massive step forward; and I think the gentlemen from Corrymeela pointed out one of the ways forward in bringing people of different traditions together in a positive and constructive way, so that they can debate the cultural diversity of the music, and debate it in a productive way.

Piers Hellawell, Queen's University of Belfast

The Orange music has a great sound, no matter what it means, and maybe some people who play music in Orange parades carry a certain message, and maybe some people just like the sound of it: I don't know. It's something we can't ignore, but at the same time, people are rejecting music for no other reason than its connotations. I have sometimes illustrated points from classical with traditional Irish musical materials when I am teaching because they illustrate the points I am trying to make, and I have never encountered any problem with that from the students, except for the one time that I do remember a student saying, 'I would never have anything to do with that kind of music!' and I said, 'Why not?' and he said, 'It is against my religion.' As a simple Englishman, I found it very strange. I didn't understand how religion had got into it at the time, but of course, it wasn't anything to do with the fact that he didn't like the music: the musical properties were there. So, I think there are really two ways in which we can perceive the music: we are going to like what it sounds like, or we are going to hate what it sounds like.

OPEN FORUM

With:
Cathal Goan
Traditional music producer, RTE

Fintan Vallely
Flute-player and Songwriter

Tommy Fegan, Conference Chairperson
We have all been addressing the responsibilities of the divided
society that exists in Ireland because we accept that the conse-
quences are very serious: people are dying each week in Ireland
because we have misunderstandings and misconceptions, and I
think it is a total cop out for anyone to suggest that over and above
the intrinsic value of traditional music (in all its art forms) that it is
in some way immune from that responsibility. I would like to
encourage everyone to seriously address this issue, namely, the
reason why we are here.

The title of the conference is 'Traditional Music: Whose Music?'
It is not 'Traditional Music: *My* Music!' or '*Our* Music!' If this was
simply a weekend to enjoy ourselves and for self-indulgence in
how wonderfully righteous we all are in being promoters of the
music, then I certainly wouldn't have wasted my time and energy
and the limited resources of Co-operation North. It is serious,
difficult, awkward and embarrassing. If it wasn't, then we wouldn't
be here. Each and every one of you are very responsible and busy
people, and I presume you are here for exactly the same reason.
You could be doing a lot of other things with your Saturday
morning rather than sitting here, so I think you owe it to yourselves, to each other, not to fudge the issue. It is awkward and it is
very delicate. I don't know what is going to come out of the
weekend. We are certainly not going to solve any problems, but we
have a serious responsibility to set a dialogue in motion – wherever

it leads – in order to try to address the issue, because we all live on the island and we are all part of it. There is no opting out. With that said, I will hand you over to Cathal.

Cathal Goan
I would like to say that I haven't the remotest idea of what you were talking about Tommy! I must say, my impression is that traditional music is about individuals meeting each other and playing music; it is not some amorphous sort of thing you can talk about. It is about individuals who meet each other and who play music; people meet all the time and play music. You can't come along and abstract the whole thing and then talk about its contribution to solving the North's problems. It is like everything else in the North: on an individual level, people do things to each other. I don't see how traditional music, anymore than a whole lot of other things in society, can be held up to some serious examination set in the context of why Provos shoot people or why the UVF shoot people. I don't think the two things come together in the slightest. If, however, we want to talk about traditional music and people's understanding of it, I am certainly prepared to do that. Would anybody like to make a comment?

Fintan Vallely
One of the things that arose yesterday, which is the nitty-gritty of the uncomfortable side of any gathering like this, is the question of the accessibility of traditional music. If you're involved in traditional music, you would realise that most of the venues for traditional music are almost exclusively, totally neutral venues. I don't know what *Comhaltas* does in the North of Ireland (maybe the venues are compromising), but I don't think that there is anybody involved in music here today who is going to say that *Comhaltas* represents them. In fact, *Comhaltas* is the symptom, the end result of some of the problems that are going on in Ireland at the present time! In my opinion, they are a self-appointed pan-Catholic organisation who take on all sorts of cultural trappings. Now, that has nothing to do with music. All of us who play music have written letters to the paper, have objected, have been thrown out of things; we have made ourselves very unpopular with *Comhaltas* down through the years, and in my mind the vast majority of musicians that I know are just left cold with the type of stuff that goes on with *Comhaltas*!

That said, *Comhaltas* certainly plays a function in music, and they do get a lot of people involved in it; and as far as I can see, *Comhaltas* is a bit like religion. My only experience of religion (or of dropping out of it) is the Catholic religion. People come into it and they learn to play music as kids. If they get a bit more enlightened and they go on to play music, they will drop out of it inevitably: I can assure you of that, because no one can tolerate being contained in that wee box! So yes, if there is a problem in traditional music it is only to do with that perception of *Comhaltas*, but I would emphasise what Cathal has said: that has nothing to do with the vast majority of people playing music. It is a facilitatory organisation.

Billy Fegan, Solicitor
In the main, it is tradition. It is part of what we are. In 1950, for example, there might have been a handful of people playing music in Ireland, and *Comhaltas* was the vehicle by which the music was brought back into a generation. That is true! No one in 1950 would have suggested, would have dreamt, that the music would have attained the level that it's at today, and I would suggest that the main vehicle for this was *Comhaltas*. They were the ones that organised the *Comhaltas' Fleadh* competitions (which I don't agree with myself, personally). *Comhaltas* is there! It's a crack of light, and it isn't going to go away. From what's been said here over the two days, I somehow get the feeling that *Comhaltas* has been knocked left, right, and centre. It's like saying that the GAA shouldn't exist!

Cathal Goan
There is a big difference between the GAA and *Comhaltas*, in that Gaelic games are only played through the GAA because they invented them (well, they invented the way they're played: fifteen men). *Comhaltas* didn't invent Irish music! There is a major difference there.

Janet Harbison, Ulster Folk & Transport Museum
In response to the *Comhaltas* thing: I feel that yesterday we had a tremendously critical session, and obviously I accept all the points. They are all tremendously valid. The fact is that *Comhaltas* has been a kind of potboiler. However, an enormous number of even the more prominent musicians here had an enormous amount to

do with *Comhaltas* in their own development. I suggest *Comhaltas* has a role; but you are dead right: the problem is that the top level of *Comhaltas* is politicised, and that is the level seen by the outsiders rather than the insiders, because that is the official face of *Comhaltas*.

John Walker, Central Community Relations Unit, Stormont

I think there are a whole lot of issues to be addressed at this conference, and you could have an agenda a mile long; but one of the things which I would like to have seen addressed (and in this respect I agree with Tommy Fegan) is that whether or not you accept it, or like it or not, to a large majority of the Protestant culture in Northern Ireland, traditional Irish music is divisive. It is seen as something that belongs to a different culture. It belongs to a Catholic culture, and not necessarily a culture which the Protestant group wants to belong to. Now, they can appreciate it and they can join in, but they don't necessarily want to become part of it! And yet, they feel excluded from it. Now, my belief is this: traditional musicians, like yourselves, have a responsibility to address that point.

Michael Longley, Arts Council of N.Ireland

Yesterday, it was said that 'musicians are part of society, therefore they are part of the problem, therefore they might be part of the solution.' Now, I think that's an enormous burden to put on any art form whether it be drama, literature, painting, or traditional music. The role of the arts in society is such a complicated and gradual thing. I mean, if our society in twenty to thirty years time is a healthier society than it is now, I am quite sure that a healthy, outgoing, generous, big-hearted traditional music movement will have made a contribution; but how one actually legislates or plans for that, I think it is impossible to say (and probably dangerous to try to do something?)

John Walker

I accept, Michael, that to say it is part of society, part of the problem, part of the tradition, is nice and glib and simple; but it's not that simple! I go back to what one of the panel speakers said yesterday, that traditional musicians have a contribution to make to addressing some of the divisions in this society. Now, I think this is a central theme and a central issue.

Fintan Vallely
Could I take that back now to the point where it was raised
yesterday; that somehow *we* have been put on the spot and the
onus has been put on us. There is something which I tried to
extract from Leslie yesterday: there is a folk memory which is not
very old (and it is Nigel, the sound-man from Aughnacloy who
reminded me of it again last night), and he says that as a child he
remembers going to dances in the Orange Hall in Aughnacloy,
and the music being played was the jigs and reels (and Leslie will
recall the same experience; and, indeed, it is possibly still going
on); and that is something that, up to a certain point in time,
people all over this island and in Scotland did. They made their
own entertainment, and there was a huge sale of accordions and
fiddles and things like that, and the music played had to be the
same, because people didn't have radios, cassettes, record- players
– well, there was the odd one, but not too many – and they made
music, and the music they made was all the same. The advent of
television killed that throughout *all* communities.

   Now, the thing is this: when the revival of the music was taking
place (and it was taking place because of the musicians themselves, not some organisation. *Comhaltas* is not an absolute organisation. *Comhaltas* is only a collection of individuals at any one point
in time), the revival possibly coincided with the re-emergence of
the Troubles; and at that point in time, I suppose, Catholics had
more identity with the South, so the revival was more open to
them: the revival wasn't open to Protestants because of that. I am
saying to you that there is music there, and if you look back, I think
there is a responsibility on you to look back into your past and talk
to your elders about music. The music was there with you as well:
why don't you attempt to seek out the roots of that (a lot of work
has been done by Sean Corcoran and Desi Wilkinson in this field)
and re-explore it from that angle? Explore your own tradition,
rather than expecting and asking us as musicians to provide the
goods for everybody! I am not saying you shouldn't ask us, but we
feel that we are being reasonably impartial. We are just playing
music, full stop, with no political trappings.

Lewis Singleton, Ulster Society
Fintan says that it is up to the people, the majority of the Ulster
Protestant community to examine their tradition. As far as we are
concerned here, we feel that there has been a failure to recognise

that there are two ethnic traditions; and we would argue from that: that whereas there may be common ground between the music of the two traditions and an interdependency, an overlap, such as the jigs and the reels and the type of dances that have been mentioned, at the same time there are certain musical aspects which are peculiar to each tradition, and I feel that a mistake has been made in that we have been talking about traditional Irish music. What you have been trying to say, what some people have been trying to say, is that there is one batch of music which is common to everyone, and everyone should somehow fit into that!

Yesterday, someone said that there is a problem with venues, that traditional Irish music will not be played at certain venues, and someone quoted the example of Markethill (which is my home town) and the Shankill. But the reality is, whether you like it or not, whether you want to face up to it or not, the majority of people in Markethill from my community do not regard traditional Irish music as their traditional music! Now, they can appreciate it, adopt it, they can enjoy it like we did last night; but at the same time there isn't a heart-and-soul affinity with it. You cannot force people to have that affinity if it is not there, and I think there has been a failure to recognise that; and it has to be recognised, and once you recognise that there are two ethnic traditions, that there is music which is solely peculiar to those traditions, then the task is to find the common ground between the two musical traditions and concentrate on that. But you can't try to force it all into one tradition.

Cathal Goan
Certainly, one of the things I was trying to say is that I would disagree that there are two traditions. I think that there are, as Sean Corcoran said yesterday, hundreds of traditions in this country; and there may well be music which is peculiar to the Unionist tradition in the North of Ireland, but there are equally tunes peculiar to Kerry and Cork, and they have different ways of playing things, they have different terms of reference in their music than perhaps the music of east Galway or north Donegal. It is when people try to make exclusive definitions that we are in danger of getting into problems. I think at least, we should talk about this music as an inclusive rather than an exclusive music. 'If it is a march it can't be a traditional tune!': if *we* adopt this attitude, then that's where we get into problems. It is after all, as Fintan said,

about people playing music. I think it is about people saying, 'I like that tune. I'd like to play it.'

Lewis Singleton

I have to disagree with what you have said and with what Sean Corcoran said yesterday. I mean, it's been said that if there is one tradition, then there are a thousand traditions, and in that same way that the tradition of a Kerry man playing traditional Irish music is in the same field of traditional music as that of an Ulster Protestant playing his form of Irish traditional music. I mean, the reality is – and this has to be recognised – OK, you can argue (as someone said to me last night) if there are a thousand traditions, 998 of them don't count: there's only two that count!

Fintan Vallely

Are we not getting into the problem of talking about cultural traditions as opposed to musical traditions? You see, the terms of reference of the conference brochure are possibly misleading. I mean, we are none the wiser about what we are supposed to be talking about than you are, or anyone else is; but I would assume, despite the inclusion of the lambeg drum on the cover of the brochure, I would assume that what traditional music means is the type of music which was revived in the '60s and has become commercially acceptable up to the point where it is an included item in pop music: the jigs and reels. I would assume that we are talking about jigs, reels, the dance music, and song, which were all equally shared – and I am adamant about this – by Protestants and Catholics here, just as the same music, in a slightly different form, is shared by people in Scotland. Possibly, some of the Scottish people present would bear that out? When your position was being stated yesterday, basically, the type of music that you considered to be traditional music was that of the Orange bands: that's fine, but it is not the Orange bands that we are talking about. I am not criticising the Orange bands, I am just saying that doesn't seem to me to be what we are talking about.

Michael Longley

OK, it is simplistic to talk about the 'two traditions', but the island is divided into two, and for the sake of argument let's talk about two traditions. It seems to me that an exclusively Orange ethos is inadequate and an exclusively Green ethos is inadequate, and both in a dangerous way are mirror images of the other. Now, we have that on the one hand, on the other hand we don't want a kind of melding together, and instead of Orange and instead of Green – and this is very crude – we have a kind of toneless grey, so I suppose one of the things we are trying to talk about at this conference is how the two traditions – OK, over-simplified – how they can prosper, be themselves and benefit from each other.

Constance Short, Co-operation North
I just want to say that I am finding the conversation a bit difficult; because, certainly as I see it, any kind of folk music should be acceptable. I know there were definitions provided for it not being called 'folk'. I know that yesterday somebody said that we aren't supposed to call traditional music 'folk music'; but I think that any kind of folk music, wherever it comes from and whatever way it grows, lives and comes out, that it should be acceptable. If some-body gets up and says, as this man said, 'My music comes out of my nationalist tradition', I think that that should be perfectly accept-able; and if this man from the Ulster Society says, 'My music and my feeling comes out of my utter Britishness, without any Irish dimen-sions', that has to be OK as well! I mean, we could get into some very complicated ground if we talk about trying to slot people into something. I really think that, more than anything else, we should be able to accommodate absolutely anything that anybody wants to describe themselves as being. If somebody considers an Orange band to be their traditional music, is that not all right?

Fintan Vallely
Yes, but there is no dispute about Orange bands. I realise that I am largely ignorant of the intricacies of the Orange band music, even though I like it and listen to it and I buy tapes of it all the time, but I am largely ignorant of it! There is no clamour by the people who are involved in the jigs and reels side to get into the Orange bands (and I am adamant that the jigs and reels are as much part of the Protestant tradition as the Catholic tradition in the North of Ireland). We are not complaining: we can't go to where the bands parade and the bands play. Therefore, that is not the issue, and there is no dispute about it. The only thing that has been said about the band music, in fact, is that we all like it, because it is all part of what we grew up with. We just like it. It may have political associations for us but, nevertheless, we can agree to like it, or

whatever. The dispute is not about that; the dispute is about this other music. That's all I am saying, and that is why I'd like somebody like Leslie, Nigel, or Desi to enlighten us on that very subject.

Dick Mac Gabhann, UU Magee
And the implication surely is that the Protestant musical tradition is larger somehow, in some respects, than the Orange band tradition; and it is this other kind of residual element that is in question. I personally have no problems about acknowledging a distinctive Protestant musical tradition, but I would be very curious to know how it is characterised. I would be very curious to know how it is defined, and from that definition how it is distinguished from the other musical traditions which exist within the country. Just this morning, I was fingering through the collection of Orange ballads that are on sale in the foyer, and I couldn't help but notice that with many of them you had perfect examples of internal rhyming schemes that are directly inspired from the Gaelic verse traditions of the province. Presumably that is part of this Protestant music tradition. It is also part of the Catholic, or nationalist, music tradition. How do you make the distinction? What are the characteristics of this tradition that make it stand separately from the other?

David Bushe, Ulster Society
If you hear a good tune you put the words to it, and you have to make the words, you have to rhyme the words to fit the tune. It is as simple as that, and the thing that people seem to be saying here is that because everybody plays the same tunes, or the same tunes are involved in both traditions, therefore they must come from the same root right the way back. There seems to be a whole sense of that here! But I mean, I can hear; and as I said last night, we are all wearing shoes, that is a connection between us, but it doesn't make one person the same as another person! People have been going on about the fact that a lot of the tunes are the same: and that is true. A lot of the tunes are the same, but in *our* traditional music it is the song that is important. To a certain extent the tune is the carrier of the song, but it is the words of the song that's important. Nobody has said that today or over the two days. It's the actual words of the song! It doesn't even matter what you sing them like, it's the words of the song that's the important thing to people.

Lewis Singleton

If I can come back, this gentleman over here said that the organi-sation we were talking about isn't represented [*Comhaltas*], that people in that organisation feel that their expression of music is part of the expression of their Irish, Gaelic, nationalist identity: we can live with that. I have no problem with that. If that is the way they want to use their music that's fine, and if we want to use our music in a similar way that's fine; but we feel that's fair enough. You accept that as your base point and then you go on to find if you like the non-contentious grounds, the grounds we do share in common, and share those and explore those. I feel, and I still feel, that there has been an underlying ethos here that it is really all part of one tradition. It isn't! The gentleman over here, when he plays his music he plays it for a different reason from the reason that I play mine. In a sense he is expressing a different identity. Once you accept that then you can go on to find the tunes that you can play together which are non-contentious, and that's the view I would take.

Desi Wilkinson, Flute-player

If you put a picture of Adolf Hilter in front of it and have Elvis Presley singing it in the sidelines, then you can do anything with it! I thought we were talking about traditional dance music and who it belongs to? It belongs to anybody who wishes to play it. It's accessible to anybody who wishes to play it and listen to it. I have no problem. If people want to march up and down and people want to do what they like, or they think they are expressing their nationalism by playing a traditional tune, that is fair enough! Everybody plays for different reasons. They might play the same music, they might play it for different reasons; but I would just like to say that traditional dance music in my experience (I can only speak from my own experience. Maybe other people have come to it from God knows where?), that it didn't belong to any one section of the community. The people I learnt it from and the people I played it with from about fourteen years old belonged to both religious groupings. I am not so sure about 'ethnic purity'! I think we are in really dangerous territory, and I don't think anybody sitting in this room here is ethnically part of one group alone. I think we are a product of the Vikings and the Normans and God knows what, and I think we should be really careful in talking about 'two ethnic groups'.

John Chilvers, Corrymeela

We have three working hypotheses: one is that there is one tradition, one is that there are two traditions, and one is that there are one thousand and two traditions. All those hypotheses are equally true and need invoking simultaneously according to our analysis of any particular situation that we find ourselves in. I want to rise to the original challenge that was made with the opening remark from Co-operation North, and then to you Cathal in disagreeing so strongly. I want to take those two together, and I think that both are actually simultaneously true because we are all here as musicians, we are all here as citizens, we are all part of the problem, and we are all potentially part of the solution no more or no less than anybody else. But surely part of the question of this conference is: how we, as musicians – the motley crew that we are, from various backgrounds – are actually going to start to do something towards helping the situation forward?

As Michael Longley was saying, it is very difficult to see how you can legislate towards this; and, in a sense, I am not sure that any kind of legislation, any kind of institutional argument, any kind of argument about the definition of the different classes of music, is necessarily going to help us. I think the answer does come back to Cathal. I think that we have now got to examine what we do when we meet together and play music, who we meet with, what our attitudes towards each other's music are when we do meet; and to what extent we broaden each other, and to what extent we restrict each other, by the way in which we treat the music that we are treating and by the way in which we treat the company that we are treating. This brings in questions to do with symbolic significance. We need to accept that the other person's position is actually genuine, and that the other person's tradition of music (even though it may be totally alien to us for political, personal, or accidental reasons) is actually genuine and authentic. So, we need to discipline ourselves to accept that authenticity, to go out and meet that authenticity, and to do some work on it for ourselves in order to be sure that we cease to see that music always as being symbolic of something else.

There is a lot of work involved in doing that in terms of personal discovery, not in terms of institutional legislation. Then, within that, the explanation to do with the unity of traditions and the inter-relationship of traditions is of great help in melting down that kind of a thing. We also need to do the other sort of a thing, namely, interpreting our music in a way which is acceptable and non-threatening to the other person that we are with, so that the next time the other person comes across our music they remember our humanity in carefully sharing it with them in a way which was respectful of them, and we remember their humanity in the way that we endeavoured to share their music respectfully; and that is the overriding thing the next time we each encounter that music. I mean, that really is how we were all introduced to the particular kinds of music that we are most enthusiastic for, as well as the things that we are not so enthusiastic for; but it is a case of getting past that barrier of fear: that area of symbolic alienation that does go with so many things and which contributes to the firing of the divisions, whether it's two divisions or one thousand and two divisions. I am sure that that is the kind of mechanism that we must begin to dedicate ourselves to, rather than planning things on an institutional level.

Fintan Vallely
I have played Irish music a lot, both inside and outside the country, and I just play it! I didn't come from a background in music, but because I began to play it, I got hooked on it. I know a lot of Scottish musicians who play Scottish music, and the music they gravitate to when playing in sessions is Irish traditional music; and I have no doubt that they get every bit of intensity from playing those tunes as the person in Kerry, Clare, or Antrim.

Cathal Goan
Isn't there a danger, in talking about this music, of an assumption that it is the most popular form of music? It is a minority taste, even among the Nationalists, the 'Irish' side of it! It is a music which is not that widespread, although it is more widespread now than it was in the past, but it doesn't have this universal appeal that it is somehow being invested with here.

Ciarán Mac Mathúna, RTE
To me, traditional music is a single musician playing for another musician. The problems come when you start to organise music. If you go back to the eighteenth century, the accounts we have of the musical evenings held in houses, big and small, show that religion and politics never entered into it. You had harpers playing with

pipers playing with fiddle-players: but these were individual per-
sons! Now, the problem arises when music emerges from a specific
political or religious background, or when a common heritage is
hijacked by a particular religious or political environment; and to
try to sort all of these things out, you have to decide whether the
music was hijacked or whether it emerged naturally within a
certain group. Obviously, certain lots of music emerged from the
Protestant tradition in the North, and the same in the South; but
there is, in my belief, a common heritage which has to do with
individual musicians meeting. Our real problem comes when you
start to organise that for political and religious ends, and if we
can't sort that out then it's not much good talking about it! The
individual musician is really the core of all tradition. For instance,
Dennis Murphy playing the fiddle: you can't separate the fiddle
from the person, or the person from the fiddle. The same with
Seamus Ennis. That is the important core of traditional music, not
the organised thing.

Cathal Goan

It seems to me (and I don't want to get into an argument about
Comhaltas, but just about Irish music) that the comment about
dilution relates to the way that Irish music has evolved over the
past couple of centuries. Some of the music we play today, some of
the more popular dances came in through the British Army bar-
racks: the lancers, which are danced all over the country. If you
want to start talking about it in terms of dilution, then maybe we
should go back to about 1820 and decide that we're not going to
play those dances any more because they came from something
outside. The fact is, it is there! The music is an organic thing. It
grows. People do things with it. They play tunes in different ways;
and to look at it in some absolute way, diluted or not, is a serious
misunderstanding of what the music is.

Fintan Vallely

It strikes me that what appears to be crystallising out of this is that
there is, on the one hand, the position stated by the Ulster Society;
and it seems to be increasingly clear that they actually like the
business of clean-cut, clear identities for the Orange band traditions and the Orange party songs. And *Comhaltas*, by their absence,
has decided that there is another partiality there. But I think there
are political songs on both sides. I am interested in *the music* as the

overview. Whereas, the man from Corrymeela seemed to be suggesting that there is a *political* overview which incorporates the music.
What we, the panellists, seem to be arguing is that there is an
impartiality of music which can override, and which has to stay
clear of any, political associations however innocuous or benign or
harmless.

Lewis Singleton

The gentleman over there said that we were also pointing the
finger at them [*Comhaltas*]. We haven't pointed the finger at
them! We are probably the only people who haven't pointed the
finger at them at this conference. We can live with their attitude as
long as they can accept our right to do the music in our way, but I
am not sure that they can.

Piers Hellawell, Queen's University of Belfast

What has struck me about the singing which we heard here yesterday is the overriding unity of experience. I haven't seen anything
divisive in these songs at all. What the Scottish repertoire, in
particular, has taught us is that most of these songs (and the songs
that Mairéad was singing last night) are celebrating a common
experience of life. I would have thought that was a source for some
kind of unity. If the music is just the message, the carrier of the
song (obviously there are political songs in both traditions), then
what we are hearing here are songs about love and unrequited
love. So, this is a common celebration: it is a celebration of life and
love, and that's something we should be learning from our Scottish visitors.

Billy Fegan

There are lots and lots of songs from, shall we say, the nationalist
side and the loyalist side. If I were to sing a song from the nationalist side, a rebel song, it would offend the people here, so everybody was very polite here yesterday. They were singing these songs
about unrequited love because they were not going to offend
anybody.

Cathal Goan

I think that is a serious misrepresentation of the people who are
here. Ask Mairéad how many rebel songs does she know!

Billy Fegan

We are talking about perceptions. Those which celebrate a famous nationalist victory or, more often, a famous nationalist defeat could be construed as being rebel songs; and the person singing those songs would in no way want to offend, so you have to choose the type of songs you sing so as not to offend in mixed company. That's really what I think part of the problem is: it's not the song or the music itself that is rejected by one party or the other, it is the person, or the history, or politics which is being either rejected or accepted. You can go into (as I have done) what is called a 'Protestant environment', sit down, and bring out your instrument and have a tune, an Irish traditional tune: that's accepted because the people in that particular situation would know me and accept me for what I am, warts and all, but if a stranger were to come in and play Irish traditional music he would be frowned upon; it might even lead to some sort of trauma. So, it is the rejection of the person rather than the music. As Ciarán Mac Mathúna said, 'You cannot separate the musician from his instrument', for if you accept the musician then you will accept his music!

Fintan Vallely

Nobody seems to be disputing the right of political party songs to exist: they exist in every single culture of the world. They exist in societies where the problems are class rather than ethnic or nationalist. They have the right to exist, but the sort of musicians that I know, generally speaking, rebel songs are not part of *their* repertoire, and the Protestant musicians who play jigs and reels and things, the Orange songs are not part of *their* repertoire. I don't think there is any dispute about that at all. I think we are getting very confused about the title: 'Whose Music?' I mean, I have no desire to spend my life playing music and being involved in sessions where there is a percentage of Orange songs and a percentage of Wolf Tone songs (or rebel songs). I like all those things in their own right, but it is not my perception of what music is about. Those are the popular expressions of music, and people are entitled to do whatever they like with them! In very broad-minded circumstances and situations we can enjoy people doing it, but we know that if you cross the dividing line in certain, unknown company, as you say, you'd get your head kicked in for singing those songs! To me, they are not part of the art side of music, and that's what I keep on wanting to address myself to.

Aodán Mac Póilin, ULTACH Trust

There have been three groups here: there is one group that talks about an Orange tradition (*their* music; *your* music is everything else); there is another group, which isn't represented, but which basically looks upon Irish music as an expression of Irish national and cultural identity; and then there is a big crowd, the vast majority of people who happen to be here, who argue that Irish music belongs to everybody, or *should* belong to everybody. This is basically Fintan's position. It is a deeply political position, in fact it is so deeply political that he claims not to know any political songs!

I have known people who have taken the same stand as Fintan in the past, and sometimes it has been a very courageous stand to take. It was quite a small minority at one stage: in the early to middle '60s that is. The whole traditional music revival at that time in the cities was dominated by Republicans and Lefties; and everybody knew that! You walked into the pubs, and you had all these people in beards, when people didn't wear beards! *Comhaltas* developed that into a kind of GAA equivalent, with a certain amount of political and cultural baggage. However, there was a large group of some of the best musicians, especially in the North, who resisted that strongly, and they had a very hard time resisting it! The Derry and Antrim fiddlers split off from *Comhaltas*, which again was itself a deeply political act. Now, those people have actually created a space for music, where music could be enjoyed by anybody from any background. Some people seem to be suggesting that traditional musicians aren't doing enough to make the music accessible to people from the unionist tradition, and Fintan has been reacting quite strongly against that, because that space has actually been created: the problem is that nobody knows about it very much. The vast majority of the urban population of Northern Ireland don't know that that space exists, which is actually one of key questions that we haven't addressed yet.

Will Glendinning, N.Ireland Community Relations Council

Can I just agree with what Aodán is saying, because I think that if you are saying that things are not political, not party political, that is a political statement because, I'm sorry, the country is divided and people do take different views. That's one of the things which we in the Community Relations Council are interested in, namely, trying to see if we can assist people who are interested in music in creating those spaces, either from a cultural point of view (a cultural traditions point of view), whether it be Irish music or whatever sort of music, or indeed people who are interested in jazz or any other type of music. We are interested in helping to create those spaces so that more people can come and can mix and join and learn about the traditions, and can learn that they don't have to take the baggage (whatever that baggage happens to be). That is the problem that I see: people from the Protestant tradition think they have to take the music and the baggage, the same way, as Aodán said, as with the Irish language. The point is that there are Protestants coming to learn the Irish language, and they are realising it is quite possible to learn the Irish language without taking the nationalist bit with it. One can learn Irish but still remain a Unionist. You don't have to automatically become a Nationalist because you learn Irish, you don't have to become a Nationalist because you enjoy traditional music; and one of the things that I found – as someone who, for instance, has been at Belfast Folk Festivals and things like that, and who was recognised as someone coming from the Protestant tradition – when I met people who were 'political' enjoying the music, was them saying 'It's great to see you are here enjoying *our* music', and what they were saying politically was that it *wasn't* mine! I mean, what you are saying politically is that it *is* mine. It was presumptuous of them to say that to me, and it is only now that I realise that it was presumptuous. I do want it to be mine, but I want it to be mine in that I want to be able to be part of Irish music, but it doesn't mean that I have to take everything else with it. That's what I am saying.

Roy McFaul, SEELB

The fact of the matter is the statement made yesterday, namely, that the music is for people who want to listen, play, or dance to it. I come from Larne, where they have what they call Irish festival dancing. Now, the people who do Irish festival dancing in the Larne and mid-Antrim area are totally mixed: they are not Catholic teams and Protestant teams. The teams are totally mixed, but it is Irish jigs and Irish reels that they dance to, and they don't feel that they are making any political statement or showing any political loyalty in any way. The music is there, and that is the music they dance to; and they certainly feel no bones about it! I think we need to get back to that idea, that the music is there for the people who want to listen, play, or use it in some form.

Cathal Goan

Thanks very much. There have been a variety of opinions expressed here over the past couple of days, and I would just like to go back to the one that I mentioned yesterday about the woman who got up in the middle of the night to sing her song because that was the time she wanted to sing. It was her, it was about her, it was her music and she wanted to do it at her time, when it suited her; but it was an expression of individualism, and I think that's what it is about. It's about individuals meeting each other and enjoying each other, and I hope that it stays that way! I would like to ask Michael Longley to finish up for us all now.

SUMMARY

With: Michael Longley

Combined Arts Director for the Arts Council
of Northern Ireland

MICHAEL LONGLEY

Everyone yesterday began with a testimony, as it were, a bit like an Alcoholics Anonymous meeting: how they first got into Irish music. My mum and dad came from Clapham Common in 1927, and I was born in Belfast in 1939. I didn't really know anything about Irish music until I was about twenty- three or twenty-four, when poetry introduced me to Seamus Heaney, who introduced me to David Hammond and various musicians. I just think that I was unlucky: all the people who grew up among songs with aunts and grandmothers learned songs before they could even read! They were lucky, but they are not superior to me, just lucky. When I was thirty I joined the Arts Council, and I founded the Literature Programme there, and then after a year or two I realised they were doing nothing for traditional music, and I started the programme for traditional music.

Brian O'Donnell's name was mentioned a few times yesterday, and it was through Brian that I launched a kind of dry run in the Arts Theatre. Brian was rather erratic, so it was a mixed menu. There was some very good music and some not so good, and what happened was – one of the most exciting moments in my life – there was a queue of people to get in right the way round to the Regency Hotel. I think this was an important moment, when an organisation like the Arts Council decided to take traditional music seriously. This was probably the first event, though, that the Arts Council Officer who had been organiser wasn't allowed into the theatre, because Brian was so under the weather that Hibbie Wilmot of the Arts Theatre wouldn't let him in! So, I had to decide between seeing the concert or looking after Brian's dignity: and I opted for the latter.

We then put on a number of tours. Again, I felt that if I could manage those tours, really I could manage anything! In fact, in those days Irish music was launched – tended to be launched – on a tidal wave of alcohol. I have noticed Ballygowan Water taking over more and more among the younger musicians, and I think this is a very good thing; but anyway, after considerable liver damage, round about 1975, I handed over to Ciarán Carson (who unfortunately can't be here, but as you know, this has been a marvellous week for him. He won the £10,000 poetry prize from the *Irish Times*-Aer Lingus competition, and he and his wife have just had a baby daughter, so a round of applause for Ciarán!).

We were the first Arts Council in these islands to do anything for traditional music. We were followed later by Dublin and Edinburgh. Every penny that I have secured for traditional music has been an uphill fight. Do write into the Arts Council and tell them that they should be spending more on it!

Two or three stories, anecdotes, from those days before I try and sum up the conference yesterday. I took a group of very good musicians for a fortnight's tour in 1972–73 when there had been a very bleak period of tit-for-tat killings. There had been an IRA atrocity in a certain town, and that's where the session was going to be played. There's no point in preaching to the converted all of the time. I took the musicians into the function room of a bar, and the bar owner said, 'My bar will be blown up unless you begin the concert or end the concert with "The Queen".' I said to him, 'I have never heard "The Queen" played on the Irish pipes!' I was thinking of cancelling: the bully boys were out, there was definitely menace in the air, so, thinking quickly I said, 'Do you have a Jimmy Shand type box-player?' because I had a vague memory that there was such a Jimmy Shand type box-player who could end the concert with some Scottish dance music and 'The Queen'. This guy turned up, and I offered him a fee. The concert went on, the audience talked through it: the Gents, I remember, was at the side of the stage, and extraordinarily large men kept lumbering threateningly backwards and forwards glaring at the musicians. But we went ahead! David Hammond, I remember, sang every Scottish song he could think of. The box-player eventually played Scottish melodies, but by the time he got round to 'The Queen', I am ashamed to say, we had all departed in our motor cars. Now, perhaps that was running away from the problem, but I had visions of Joe Burke's fingers being broken and so forth.

On another occasion, at the request of the UDA, we put on a small concert of Irish music in their headquarters in east Belfast. I was out of Belfast at the time, but that went very well and great interest was shown in the music. John Morrow, my colleague, talked about the musicians going into the HQ there 'like Egyptologists descending into the tomb!' Anyway, apparently it was a success, and that is perhaps the sort of thing we should be doing?

Another story has to do with trailing around Donegal with Brian O'Donnell in search of the great Johnny Doherty, whose name I was glad to hear mentioned here yesterday. Johnny was still on the road in those days, although he was over seventy, and even in old age still the itinerant musician: a fiddler of great genius! After about two or three days we eventually tracked him down to a little pub where he was playing away. He was being patronised, and everyone was talking through the music. Brian and I sat behind him, and we must have been an oasis of silence because when he had finished his first set he turned round very slowly and nodded in the most dignified fashion in our direction. I have often thought, as a bureaucrat that is the least I can try to offer, an oasis of that kind of respect.

Just a final anecdote. Because Brian was very fond of her, I took the rash move in the second tour of employing Maggie Barry who calls herself the 'Singing Gypsy Woman'. I always thought, even when Maggie was singing 'When Irish Eyes are Smiling', that there was something authentic about her: and I ended up loving her personality. In Armagh I realised that the Protestant Primate, George Simms, was sitting in the front row, and Maggie had been getting raunchier as the week proceeded, so I said to Maggie, 'You'll never guess who is in the front row: George Simms, the Protestant Primate of All Ireland!' That's all I said. I wasn't going to try to control her, so she came out and she started to tune her banjo, and as you know, she only played one string on it but she always made a great thing of the tuning up, and she says, 'I can't get this thing tuned at all!' she says; 'The frets are all wet and sticky, but sure that's me all over!' with an enormous wink in the direction of the Protestant Primate. Then afterwards, George came and said, 'I enjoyed the evening so much. Irish music so reminds me of the *Book of Kells*'.

Now, I come from a middle-class Protestant background. My

homeland is between the Malone Road and the Lisburn Road, just a little bit north of Balmoral Avenue; but my involvement in traditional music has been one of the most important things in my life, and after those first three or four tours I wrote a short poem which, before I do my proper summing up, I think I would like to read as an offering. It is called *Fleadh,* and it is dedicated to Brian O'Donnell, and it is five little six-line poems describing each instrument.

FLEADH
for Brian O'Donnell

Fiddle

Stained with blood from a hare,
Then polished with beeswax
It suggests the vibration
Of diaphanous wings
Or – bow, elbow dancing –
Follows the melted spoors
Where fast heels have spun
Dewdrops in catherine-wheels.

Flute

Its ebony and silver
Mirror a living room
Where disembodied fingers
Betray to the darkness
Crevices, every knothole –
Hearth and chimney-corner
For breezes igniting
The last stick of winter.

Bodhran

We have eaten the goat:
Now his discarded horns
From some farflung midden
Call to his skin, and echo
All weathers that rattle
The windows, bang the door:
A storm contained, hailstones
Melting on this diaphragm.

Whistle

Cupped hands unfolding
A flutter of small wings
And fingers a diamond
Would be too heavy for,
Like ice that snares the feet
Of such dawn choruses
And prevents the robin
Ripening on its branch.

Pipes

One stool for the fireside
And the field, for windbag
And udder, milk and rain
Singing into a bucket
At the same angle: cries
Of waterbirds homing:
Ripples and undertow –
The chanter, the drones.

Andy Crockart insisted that we stop in Augher, just for a warmer, so I am afraid I missed Sean's kick-off yesterday, but I was in time to hear David Bushe saying that 'what stirs my heart', he said, 'is our own music'. I remember being with a great Irish poet, Derek Mahon, in O'Neill's in Suffolk Street in Dublin when the Twelfth of July was being broadcast on TV. Everyone in the bar was ignoring it, and Derek and I were pretending to ignore it as well but with one eye cocked, two literary sophisticates disowning our roots; but one of those slitter-slatter bands came on, and Mahon and I beat time under the tables like this! So, as David Bushe says, it does bind people together. He said Orange *or* Green, and I suppose I would like to say Orange *and* Green. I don't think any of us wishes for a toneless melding together, a running together of the colours of orange and green into some awful boring grey! So, skill is required to keep the bracing, life-enhancing tensions from degenerating into threatening, even death-dealing, triumphalism. It is a question, really, of 'How do we substitute cultural pride for political aggression?' Orange music is part of the tradition.

To quote Tom Munnelly: he talked about 'one large jewel of many facets', and he said, 'if one facet is blurred, the jewel is diminished by its lack'; and Tom touched on many important points: the affluent move from home to pub and the effects of microphones and stages. He also referred to 'the green knee breeches approach of *Comhaltas*'. The cultural scene is complicated by politics, but complexity can sometimes be a thicket in which it is comfortable and comforting to hide. I don't know who it was who said 'simplicity is greatness', but Tom made a couple of simple, challenging remarks. He said, 'a good song is a good song', and then speaking as a collector he said, 'I am an observer of what people are doing. It is not my role to influence this.'

Then, I think, we all welcomed the presence of Piers Hellawell. I have seen Piers wrapped in concentration at sessions in Belfast, and to have him not only telling us but showing us through his music the effect that the freshness and the directness of traditional music have had on him! I think he referred to a way out of the modernist complex jungle. He talked about world music, and I found his three pieces, and especially the one to the seal, very beautiful. But I'd ask him a question – which he could answer over a drink later on – why is the noun 'synthesis' usually good and the adjective 'synthetic' usually bad?

'An Island Experience' with Flora MacNeil and Mary Jane Campbell was, for me, a magical experience; and again, it was the songs that mattered, and as Flora said, 'The songs, where they come from I don't know'. Now, she was lucky to be surrounded by songs from an early age. She said, 'I soaked them up', and then, really, the sentence that struck me the most of all yesterday was her simple phrase 'My tradition, how it happened to me'. Then Mary reminded us that it was the Catholic islands, for complicated reasons, that kept the good songs alive; there was the nightmare of the bonfire of fiddles at the end of the nineteenth century when Evangelicals from outside moved in and tried to get rid of all secular music. But this generated new songs with the Church as a strong influence. New hymns were written in Gaelic and they had a way of holding on to tunes. Love-songs were changed into psalms, which reminds one of The Saint Matthew Passion of Bach where one of the most serenely religious passages is, in fact, just a love-song from another work of his which he, in a hurry, fitted in. I wasn't too sure, but I got the impression they agreed, our two visitors from the islands, that the Catholic and Protestant musics on the islands are different aspects of a single tradition; and more than that, they are related to traditions within what John Hewitt used to call 'this archipelago'. There are similarities between the Gaelic songs and the *sean-nós* tradition, especially in the interplay of ornament and melody.

Paddy Glackin in the next session reminded us of the difficulties of traditional music in an urban context, and of learning it but not being able to relate it to anyone apart from his father. He used a lovely word, the 'tabernacle', the tabernacle of human contact which eventually built up in Dublin; but he said that the two most important days of his life were when he went to see Johnny Doherty in Donegal, and he referred to Johnny Doherty as a 'real carrier'. Then Paddy went on to question the use of competition, which is something we might have talked about this morning: about the demise of regional styles, about the little bigotries and elitisms within traditional music. He did suggest that the prognosis was good, that there were plenty of youngsters with the technique, but that what they needed was to be exposed to older people, to warmth and expression.

Desi Wilkinson: a marvellous flautist (I love calling him 'flautist' because he insists on being called a flute-player!) His story was similar. It was about human contact, about meeting Tommy Gunn in Botanic Avenue; and again, a lovely quote from Desi: he said, 'Traditional music is people in the room, relaxed and open, vibrant in their camaraderie', and he referred to the human face of the music.

Mairéad Ní Dhomhnaill provided me with a beautiful image. She talked about 'My grandmother, a quiet singer, sitting in the kitchen, the clock ticking'; and, as with Flora MacNeil, she referred to the old songs. They went in somewhere, somehow. Again, I was reminded of the blessings of being surrounded by songs from an early age, steeped in singing. Another key figure for her was an aunt who urgently wanted to pass on to Mairéad the repertoire of songs, both English and Irish.

And then, Leslie Bingham from an Orange background telling us that he plays the music simply because he loves it. And Richard Parkes, reminding us of the crossover between the Scottish and Irish traditions, the jigs and the reels that are shared. Unlike other speakers, he thought that the competitions were a good thing, but this meant that the band stood still rather than march! One of the things that I have been proud of in my job with the Arts Council is giving support to the educational programme of the Royal Scottish Pipe Band Association for over a decade, up to the point where they are now inaugurating a *Piobaireachd* Programme. I was interested to hear that Irish music played on the Scottish pipes is a trend among the young, and that at Inverness this year the top prize was won by an Irish piper playing an Irish tune on the Scottish pipes!

With the last session on 'Traditional Music: the Public Perception', the debate really quickened. Everyone spoke well, but it was Tony McAuley who grasped the nettle and suggested that the historical mess has contaminated traditional music, whether we like it or not! It was Ciaran Mac Mathuna who went on to outline briefly the political, religious, and class pressures which have sought either to diminish or control the music.

I'll just pursue the thoughts that that last session put into my mind. It is an interesting title 'Whose Music?' because it implies ownership, and that implies the question 'Should there be any ownership?' I think we all agree that the answer to that is 'No!' Nobody has been asked to give up anything, and surely everything is open.

The absence of *Comhaltas* has to be commented on. I would say, before I say anything further about them, that it has been an enormous pleasure for me in the Arts Council to work with local branches of *Comhaltas* throughout the North; but they seem to be different? The ethos is different from what you get from HQ. They are not here, in fact they held an alternative conference a few weeks ago. If this does nothing else it shows that there is a problem, and it exposes the desire of some people to package traditional music in their own ideals! As far as they are concerned, definitions have to be controlled. They decide what 'Irishness' is, and anyone who doesn't subscribe to their definition is less Irish; and I for one, with my background, hate the notion that there can be degrees of Irishness. One of the things that we can do is to resist that totalitarianism.

The ethos of the independence movement has probably unavoidably coloured both the Irish language and traditional music, and it has put people off both. It has put them off it up here in the North, but it has also put them off it in the South. Most of my Southern friends have been put off the Irish language by the various ways it has been thrust upon them, and it is the exclusivist attitude that puts people off the music as the thing itself; and that's what the music is, the thing itself! But it also falsifies the thing itself, the music; and even worse, pushes the music – or would push the music, wants to push the music – into dangerous racist areas. There are always going to be attempts to hijack something as rich and attractive and potent as our music. There will always be pressure groups – and in bed last night I asked myself, 'Are liberals like myself, the would-be peacemakers, just another pressure group?' – and the privileged status which the music has in cultural circles, I wonder if that might be bad for it? It means, perhaps, that other kinds of musical activity and expression aren't recognised. We can draw a parallel with the Gaelic games movement. Then all of a sudden Irishness was expressed perfectly, effortlessly through a successful World Cup soccer team. One of the interesting things about the Republic of Ireland's soccer team was, I gather, that it had quite a lot of support on the Shankill Road! When people are turned off things in the North of Ireland this is often a reflection of wrong or careless attitudes in the South. To like Irish music should not imply any kind of politics, and likewise to dislike it should not imply any kind of politics. I draw to a close with what has really overwhelmed at this conference, and I think it has been a good conference, and congratulations to Constance and Peter and and their colleagues for putting it on, and to all of you for coming and for the people who have performed; but what has overwhelmed me is how personal it all is, how specific. I mean, there was Mairéad's grandmother and her aunt, Desi Wilkinson meeting Tommy Gunn, Paddy Glackin's pilgrimage to Johnny Doherty, Flora MacNeil's lovely phrase: 'My tradition, how it happened to me'. When you go to any gig, any concert, the introductions are great: they are invariably along these lines, 'I got this jig from Joe so and so of such and such a townland, and he called it whatever the name is, but last week in Sligo I heard the same jig called by a different name'. It is specifics, and it is specifics spelt out in personal terms, and it is a perfect example of what the Latin root meaning of 'tradition' is: 'tradere', 'trans-dare', to hand over, to pass on. A network of these handings over, an accumulation of these handings-on is surely firstly and lastly what we should mean when we refer to the culture of the music.

We are talking about something that is intimate and at the same time vast. We have in Northern Ireland a uniquely rich confluence of English and Irish and Scottish songs and tunes; and it is that very richness which produces political problems, social complexities. But I believe, to answer John Walker's plea, that there is a possibility of redemption in the vitality and generosity of the music; and to take up Ciaran's point, Protestants used to be deeply involved in this music. It is very important for us after twenty years, twenty years of what we call 'the Troubles', to realise that things haven't always been like this and that they aren't always going to be like this. We have been here in the company of folk who are gifted and profound, custodians of a treasure-trove; looking back beyond our own history, they are contemporary exponents of the ancient Indo-European tradition of singing and story-telling; they are Homer's representatives in our midst! The great Irish poet, Louis MacNiece, said, 'The future is the bride of what has been'; here we are trying to look into the future through the eyes of the past, and I think we are beginning to do it with generosity and with bigger hearts.

Constance Short, Co-operation North
Well we have arrived at the conclusion of our conference and I want to thank you all for coming and contributing so eloquently and openly to the debate, and to the wonderful singing and playing we heard throughout the week-end.

I want to thank Michael Longley for ending on such a warm and generous and hopeful note. Let's hope that our conference will contribute something to an understanding and tolerance of the great variety of cultural expressions on this island of ours.

BIOGRAPHIES OF MUSICIANS AND CONTRIBUTORS

Leslie Bingham, from County Down, is a well-known and much-respected flute-player. He has been deeply influenced by the music of the Sligo-Leitrim area; and his enthusiasm for and love of traditional music have encouraged countless younger people. His three children: Tara, Terry, and Ciaran are all great musicians.

David Bushe, from Markethill in County Armagh, is Graphics Artist Manager with the Ulster Society (which explores and promotes Ulster-British heritage and culture), based in Brownlow House, Lurgan. He has been instrumentally involved in the publication of the Society's two song-books, *The Orange Lark* and *Lilliburlero!*, researching the songs and compiling the musical scores for them.

Mary Jane Campbell, who originally comes from the mainland, now lives on Lewis, the northernmost (and predominantly Protestant) island of the Outer Hebrides. Mary has sung and acted with the Gaelic drama group *Fir Chlis*, and she is a very fine exponent of the Scots Gaelic song tradition of the Western Isles.

Ciarán Carson is a flute-player and is the Traditional Arts Officer of the Arts Council of Northern Ireland. Ciaran is the author of the indispensable, ready-reference companion of all those interested in the wider world of traditional music: *The Pocket Guide to Irish Traditional Music*, as well as three books of poetry. He won the 1990 prize in the *Irish Times*-Aer Lingus poetry competition.

Sean Corcoran is a traditional singer and a very fine mandolin-player. He comes from Drogheda, and has been deeply involved in collecting songs and music over many years. Sean is editor of a forthcoming series of cassette and pamphlet packs of this material, *Harvest Home.*

Andy Crockart is a commissioning editor with Ulster Television, and has made many programmes exploring folk and traditional music down through the years.

Paddy Glackin is a fiddle-player whose style and repertoire has been shaped and influenced by the late and much-respected Johnny Doherty from Donegal. Formerly, he was presenter of RTE's traditional music programme, *The Long Note*.

Cathal Goan is an RTE producer and an authority on the song tradition of Donegal.

Piers Hellawell is a classical musician and composer, and someone with a very keen interest in traditional music. He is a music lecturer at Queen's University of Belfast, and has held the post of Composer-in-Residence at Queen's.

Michael Longley is the Combined Arts Director of the Arts Council of Northern Ireland, overseeing several of the Council's programmes on Literature, Traditional Music, and Community Arts. His poetry has received, and continues to receive, many accolades.

Robaird Mac Góráin, one of the founder-members of *Gael-Linn* (the Irish language and cultural organisation), is presently the Deputy Chief Executive and a member of the Board. Riobard has worked rigorously and extensively in producing records in the Irish language. He is also a member of the Board of the Irish American Cultural Institute, based in Saint Paul, Minnesota, which publishes the journal *Eire-Ireland*.

Ciarán Mac Mathúna started his career with RTE in 1954, as a producer with special responsibility for the collection and presentation of Irish folk music and folklore. He initiated seminal traditional music programmes, such as *A Job of Journeywork*. He is best known today for his *Mo Cheol Thu* programme on RTE1: a presentation of all that is best in Irish music, song, and poetry.

Flora MacNeil is internationally recognised as the leading exponent of the Scots Gaelic song tradition. Although she now lives on the mainland, Flora originally comes from Barra, the southern most (and predominantly Catholic) island of the Outer Hebrides.

Tony McAuley is a folk singer. He is a television producer with the BBC in Northern Ireland; and having spent many years working on their education programmes, now specialises in features looking at Ulster's heritage and traditions. He has recently produced the traditional music series, *The Corner House*, a joint BBC-RTE production.

Dermot McLaughlin, Music Officer with *An Chomhairle Ealaion*, learned much of his fiddle-playing in south-west Donegal and Derry.

Tom Munnelly works for the Department of Irish Folklore at University College Dublin, and is the only full-time collector of traditional song in Ireland. He has been working professionally in the field since 1971. In addition, Tom is the Chairman of both the Irish Traditional Music Archive and the Willie Clancy Summer School.

Mairéad Ní Dhomhnaill is a singer of traditional songs in both Irish and English. Her repertoire has been greatly influence by her aunt Neili Ní Dhomhnaill from Ranafast in Donegal.

Richard Parkes, Pipe-Major of the Field Marshall Montgomery Pipe Band, plays the Scottish pipes *par excellence*, bringing an apparent effortlessness to each and every performance. He has adapted many traditional Irish tunes to fit the Scottish pipes. Richard has won numerous competitions in both Ireland and Scotland, and the Field Marshall Montgomery Pipe Band have recently taken the Argyle Shield out of Scotland for the first time in the competition's history.

Fintan Vallely is a flute-player and song-writer from Armagh. He is the author of the definitive tutor for the Irish flute.

Desi Wilkinson is a flute-player who originally comes from Belfast. His style has been keenly influenced by the music of the Sligo-Leitrim area (he was awarded a bursary by *An Chomhairle Ealaion* to study the flute music of that area). At present, Desi is one of four artists in the community working under the auspices of the Arts Council of Northern Ireland.

After dinner, 'Barney McCool' made his appearance (and his presence felt) at the conference, as **Tom McDevitte**, raconteur and wit, marvellously regaled everyone with stories, both old and new, jokes, and strange insights into the workings and the ways of the old Great Northern Railway; at times deliciously outlandish, at times poignant and circumspect – never outrageous nor out of touch – but always with a watchful and a wary eye on the shenanigans and goings-on of his audience at the bar. Badinage at its best!